The
JESUS
PRINCIPLE

*Are You Moving
Toward Jesus—or Away?*

L JAMES JOHNSON

Disclaimer: The information in this book is provided for educational and entertainment purposes only. While every effort has been made to ensure accuracy and completeness, no warranty is expressed or implied. The author and publisher are not engaged in rendering legal, financial, medical, or other professional advice. Readers should consult appropriate professionals before acting on any information in this book. The author and publisher disclaim any liability for any loss or damage incurred as a consequence of the use and application, directly or indirectly, of any information presented herein. The views and opinions expressed in this book are those of the author and do not necessarily reflect the official policy or position of any affiliated organization.

Unless otherwise noted, all Scripture quotations are taken from the World English Bible.

Cover and interior formatting by KUHN Design Group | kuhndesigngroup.com

© 2025 L. James Johnson. All rights reserved.

No part of this publication may be reproduced, stored in a retrieval system, or transmitted in any form or by any means—electronic, mechanical, photocopying, recording, or otherwise—without the prior written permission of the publisher, except for brief quotations in reviews or scholarly works.

Published in the United States of America by Lone Wolf Consortium Publishing, LLC

Contact:
hello@TheJesusPrinciple.com
TheJesusPrinciple.com
substack.com/@thejesusprinciple

ISBN: 978-1-935736-14-1

ACKNOWLEDGMENTS

This book was written amid both faith and friction, shaped by the people who kept me grounded through it all. To Robyn, Lani, Carl, Brad, and Daniel—each of you helped me see the world through eyes different from my own, which may be the truest form of grace. To Maria, thank you for your patience and steady presence along the way. To Alia, whose insights offered a lens for deeper understanding. To Mike and Connie, who stayed steady through the storm. And to David Carr, whose editorial insight and encouragement left their mark even in his absence, I remain grateful.

And to all those Christians devoted to emulating the character of Jesus and providing principled resistance to the authoritarian forces seeking to destabilize our democratic way of life, your quiet courage and daily work bring light to dark places. The good you do far outweighs the bad press associated with those who misuse Christianity for nationalist ends. You deserve to be recognized and remembered with gratitude.

CONTENTS

Acknowledgments 3

Prologue: *The Jesus Principle* 7
> Kick off the journey at America's faith crossroads, where dueling Bibles and divided hearts challenge us to rediscover Jesus at the center.

1. Saints and Sinners 11
> Watch real Christians clash with conscience as compassion collides with tough decisions, shattering comfort zones and exposing moral shadows.

2. Women at the Crossroads 31
> Ride the front lines with women navigating faith, freedom, and danger as political and religious battles turn female bodies into battlegrounds, and dignity into an act of rebellion.

3. Healing or Harm: The Cost of Survival 49
> Brace yourself as American healthcare becomes a high-stakes gamble, with families tossed between heartbreak and hope, revealing just how close survival sits to the edge.

4. Justice for All 61
> Follow Jamal's dream and America's struggle, as race, class, and opportunity collide in a fight for true justice that either opens locked doors, or leaves them forever closed.

5. Who Is My Neighbor? 83

> Face the midnight knock as immigration and identity push Christian neighbors to cross lines of fear, risking comfort to rescue the vulnerable and redefine what it means to belong.

6. Stewardship or Exploitation? 99

> Breathe in the smoky air as climate crisis and creation care force faith communities to choose: will stewardship spark renewal, or will exploitation let the planet burn?

7. LGBTQ+ and the Church 119

> Step into the epic faith showdown as churches wrestle between exclusion and embrace, turning ancient texts and real lives into a crucible for dignity and radical love.

8. Christian Nationalism 137

> Expose the power plays and fiery rhetoric as politics and faith battle for the soul of America, revealing the pitfalls and promise of Christian influence in overdrive.

9. A New Paradigm 157

> Lean forward into hope, as they shake off comfort and tribe, America's Christians are challenged to build faith, democracy, and justice that look dangerously like Jesus.

PROLOGUE

THE JESUS PRINCIPLE

A NEW PARADIGM AT THE CROSSROADS

America stands at a crossroads: divided not just by politics, but by dueling Bibles and rival claims about faith, justice, and what it means to be a neighbor and Christian.

The questions we face aren't new, but the stakes feel higher. Will religion be weaponized for power and exclusion, or reclaimed as a call to inherent compassion and truth? Can we find a way that looks more like Jesus and less like culture wars?

GOOD-HEARTED SOULS

Most American Christians are good-hearted and do their best to live out their faith. Week after week, they're the ones showing up after hurricanes, staying up all night with the dying, bringing casseroles when disaster hits, and stepping up for the least of these—locally and worldwide. The church isn't just a place of debate and division; for millions, it's where people rally to serve, comfort, and carry each other through the worst of times.

Yet for all these acts of goodness and compassion, there's a growing and unavoidable rift, a disconnect between our religious beliefs and practices and the actual life and teachings of Jesus. Too often, what's preached or promoted leads people away from His core message, not toward it. That's the crisis that the Jesus Principle is designed to confront.

THE JESUS PRINCIPLE

Across these chapters, we'll explore the Jesus Principle: a simple but disruptive compass and filter for Christian life and public witness. Not a new doctrine, but a tool to cut through the noise and get back to the Gospel's heart. The Jesus Principle asks four hard questions:

- Does this bear the fruit of the Spirit—love, joy, peace, patience, kindness, goodness, faithfulness, gentleness, and self-control?
- Does this care for the vulnerable?
- Would I want this done to me—or those I love?
- Is this true—aligned with the life and teaching of Jesus, and the facts?

As a compass, the Jesus Principle points us toward compassion, justice, humility, and truth. As a filter, it sifts out toxins: fear, pride, racism, exclusion, and political tribalism poisoning both church and nation while leaving in what is sustaining and life-giving.

A NEW PARADIGM—
FORWARD, NOT LEFT OR RIGHT

At the crossroads, this book invites a new paradigm, one guided not by party lines, tradition, or tribe, but by the fierce example of Jesus.

Faith that risks comfort for love, measures itself not by who it keeps out, but how wide it opens the circle.

DIVISIVE ISSUES

In these pages we'll wrestle with America's hardest debates, including healthcare access, inequality, race, immigration, stewardship of creation, LGBTQ+ inclusion, reproductive justice, and Christian nationalism. With each, the Jesus Principle demands real answers—not easy ones—and insists on humility, honest questions, and stubborn love.

The conversation continues online and in upcoming volumes, where I'll also share how even well-meaning faith can cast moral shadows when it drifts from compassion and truth into division and scapegoating.

CHURCH, STATE, AND REAL FREEDOM

America's First Amendment protects freedom of conscience, not to erase religion from public life, but to keep faith authentic and free. The wall separating church and state is there to defend liberty for everyone, not just a vocal few. Christian nationalism risks everyone's liberty for the illusion of control. Any belief that shapes law for all deserves scrutiny.

I'm not here to ban beliefs, but I'll fight to limit harm. The Jesus Principle calls us all—especially Christians—to defend the vulnerable, live by the Golden Rule, grow the fruit of the Spirit, and serve truth, whole and unvarnished.

A CALL TO COURAGE AND HOPE

The Jesus Principle is a journey, a daily choice to move toward Christ's heart, even when it costs comfort, certainty, or familiar approval. America's story is still being written, and the biggest question isn't just the kind of nation we build, but the kind of people we're willing to become.

Will we cling to divisions and fear, or will we risk a new path—faith that looks like Jesus, politics rooted in compassion, and hope big enough for all?

The answer is ours to live.

> *Stay brave. Stay true—to yourself,*
> *your values, and our shared future.*

CHAPTER 1

SAINTS AND SINNERS

KYLER'S VOTE

The moment the motion passed, tension in the church basement snapped like a rubber band. Forty percent—gone from the church's food pantry. "Tough love," Pastor Richards called it. "Teaching people self-reliance instead of dependence."

Others nodded, but Kyler couldn't meet Emma's eyes on Sunday. Second grader. Always hungry for seconds at the potluck. Her mom clings to two jobs and still can't fill their fridge.

Kyler lies awake that night, staring at the ceiling and asking the only question that matters: Did I just use my faith to take food from a hungry child?

And the question he can feel to the depth of his soul: Did I move closer to Jesus, or further away?

THE MORAL SHOCKWAVE

Have you ever gone to bed wrestling with a decision like this? Have you wondered in the dark if your faith just put a wall up—or knocked one down—for someone in need?

If you've ever felt your Christian convictions clash with your conscience, you're not alone. That moment forced Kyler to face some brutal questions: How can resolute followers of Jesus support policies that feel so far from His compassion? What happens when our deepest beliefs about Scripture collide with the Christ we claim to follow?

Consider Jason, a deacon well-known for encouraging his family to help neighbors whenever possible. When the church cut funding for the food pantry, Jason still wanted to support those in need, but he worried about encouraging dependency. So he quietly left grocery cards for Emma's family on their porch, making sure not to sign his name so they wouldn't feel obliged or singled out.

He explained to his wife that while he believes charity should help people without making them dependent, he couldn't ignore Emma's situation. And even after acting according to his principles, Jason found himself haunted by the thought of Emma sitting in class with an empty lunchbox, wondering if he had done enough or simply eased his own conscience.

These personal struggles—where compassion collides with principle—didn't just start with one church meeting or policy change; they were seeded years earlier, shaping my own journey before I even understood how deep the divide would grow.

A STRANGER IN A STRANGE LAND

It began for me when I returned to my hometown on the prairies after turning thirty. I arrived with my wife, three kids, and two pets, expecting to reconnect with old friends and a faith I remembered as gentle and mostly private.

Instead, I discovered zeal. My childhood friends—guys I'd played hockey, football, and basketball with, girls I'd grown up alongside—were now fervent, conservative, born-again Christians. My best friend Mike and his wife Connie were all-in. Within a year and a half, they'd converted my wife, Wanda, and she proudly confirmed that she had converted the kids. Suddenly, I was a stranger in a formerly familiar land—seemingly, the only one not swept up by this new religious tsunami.

OLD FAITH, NEW FACES

When I'd left years earlier, nobody outside of the Christmas and Easter holidays talked seriously about Jesus. Now, faith dominated every conversation, shaped every relationship, and set boundaries for every decision.

But this wasn't just any faith. It was a particularly American brand of Christianity, part assurance, part anxiety. It seemed built on more rules than grace, more judgment than mercy.

I watched people, convinced they were following Jesus, act in ways that felt miles from Christlike. These were good-hearted people, doing the best they could after devoting their lives to Jesus. Yet they drew lines, built walls, claimed love, but practiced exclusion. I heard passionate sermons about loving others, but church policies often ended up excluding or hurting the vulnerable, a sharp contradiction to the compassion they preached.

For example, Emma's mother used to teach Sunday School. Then, new policies barred her, quietly but firmly, because she was raising her kids alone after her divorce. "We've got to uphold Biblical standards," the church board explained, never imagining Jesus might have done the opposite.

INCLUSION OR EXCLUSION

A blatant example is the exclusion of LGBTQ+ individuals from membership, leadership, or church sacraments. For decades, major denominations (like the United Methodist Church) enforced bans on LGBTQ+ clergy and same-sex marriage. People heard about God's boundless love, while church policy told some that their identity disqualified them from full participation.

What's striking biblically is how many churches prioritize which sins "count." In Leviticus, the same capital penalty is assigned to adultery and male same-sex acts (Leviticus 20:10 and 20:13; see 18:22). Yet in practice, many congregations minimize or overlook adultery while singling out homosexuality as a boundary-setting sin.

That inversion isn't how Jesus handled moral failure. When presented with an adulterous woman, he refused to enforce the code as a spectacle of purity, turned the spotlight to the accusers' conscience, and sent her away with mercy and a call to change (John 8:3–11). He warned against straining gnats while swallowing camels (Matthew 23:23–24) and against the plank-and-speck hypocrisy that fuels selective outrage (Matthew 7:1–5).

The pattern is hard to miss; when we prioritize sins to match our preferences, we risk projecting our personal biases onto God and then calling those biases "biblical." I call that gap a *moral shadow*, the distance between the Jesus I met in Scripture and the way I was treated in his name. I couldn't unsee it; the dissonance became a "calling." I spent years learning not only what had shifted in my hometown, but how, in practice, to tell when we're walking toward Jesus and when we're drifting away.

Have you ever come home to find your faith community changed, maybe even transformed, beyond recognition? Or felt the awkward sting of being the outsider in a place that once felt like home? If so, you know the jolt that makes you start asking new questions.

HOW THE JESUS PRINCIPLE AROSE

These questions wouldn't let me go, not in the quiet after church, and not on sleepless nights listening to the prairie winds and thunderstorms. The Jesus Principle didn't leap out of a book or a sermon. It emerged from the widening gap—this moral shadow—between the Christlike love I was taught and the realities I saw in people I cared about.

Good-hearted, earnest Christians insisted their actions came from love, but their beliefs often divided, ignored the Golden Rule, lacked humility, or turned mean-spirited, especially toward the "least of these." And all while declaring themselves Jesus's followers.

Don't get me wrong, these same friends and neighbors accomplished huge things when it came to charity and helping others. Their local churches organized food drives, built shelters, collected clothes, and showed up for the vulnerable time after time. When someone was in need—hungry, grieving, facing impossible odds—they gathered their money, time, and sweat to meet that need. At their best, they were truly "all in," loving their neighbor as themselves, sometimes in ways that amazed me. They were Christians to the core.

But at the same time, they drew boundaries that Jesus never drew. As open as their hands could be, there were still people quietly, but clearly, being left out. Often, those lines weren't traced by Christ's commands, but by fears, traditions, or rules that Jesus Himself routinely broke for the sake of compassion.

Before long, it became crystal clear: on almost every major issue in American life, there are not just two political camps, but two passionately defended Christian perspectives. Inside the church, even inside families, you'll find sincere believers standing on opposite sides, each convinced they are defending the faith.

IS IT GOD'S VOICE OR OURS?

That's when it hit me: we don't just have a problem of disagreement; we have a crisis of discernment. America doesn't need another doctrinal debate; it needs a new paradigm, something that cuts through all the claims and counterclaims, all the "we have the real truth" arguments.

The breaking point came as I watched both "sides" claim the highest ground. Born-again credentials? Both claimed spiritual rebirth. Biblical inerrancy? Both could quote Scripture for hours. Denominational authority? The body of Christ splintered at every new question.

So, who was actually following the Spirit, and who was simply parroting their tribe, projecting their own preferences onto God? I needed a new measuring stick, a compass honest enough to break through the noise.

Instead of asking if faith is about having the "right" doctrines or quoting scripture to win debates, I wondered: what if the real test for Christianity is whether our beliefs and actions actually reflect the life, character, and priorities of Jesus? If He is the center, shouldn't everything—not just theology, but politics and ethics—be measured by His example?

INTRODUCING THE JESUS PRINCIPLE

The Jesus Principle was born out of all these questions and contradictions: simple, disruptive, and necessary. Here it is, in a nutshell:

The Jesus Principle:
How Christian beliefs and practices
lead us *toward* or *away* from Jesus.

When Christians clash on a belief, policy, or action, the core question is this: Which side moves us toward the character and teachings of Jesus, and which side pulls us away?

Think about the last time you wrestled with a difficult call. Maybe it was a family argument, a political debate, or just a small moment of conscience at work or church. Did you start by searching for Jesus's heart, or did you just grab for the answer that felt safest and most familiar? Be honest: have you ever caught yourself on autopilot, not really checking in with where you stand in relation to Christ?

If that sounds familiar, you're not alone. It's easy to drift, especially when faith gets tangled with habit, tradition, or tribal loyalty. That's why something clearer, more honest is needed.

This new approach is not a doctrine; it's a lens, a filter, and a compass. When you wonder if God is speaking or if your voice just echoes your own hopes and hangups, the Jesus Principle gives you a gut-check.

REAL-LIFE ISSUES

Let's land at the kitchen table. Imagine praying for your teenage son after he comes out as gay. Your minister says it's time for tough love, and if he wants shelter at sixteen, he must obey your rules or face life on his own. In that moment, ask yourself honestly: does this move you toward the Jesus who ate with outcasts, or away from everything you know about His grace? Does "tough love" bring healing, or does it fracture what Jesus was desperate to restore?

I saw a father in our church face this after overhearing his wife weeping over their estranged daughter. They'd followed every sermon, every policy, but in that silence, he asked: did our faith build a bridge, or a wall?

The Jesus Principle isn't about easy answers or tidier debates. It's about soul-piercing honesty every time: Does this bear fruit that looks like Jesus? Does it protect the "least of these?" Is it true, or just comforting?

DUELING BIBLES AND REAL-WORLD STAKES
The Conservative Christian Perspective

Here's where things can flare up. When it comes to hungry kids in America—a basic moral fault line—Christian convictions run deep and split sharply.

Conservative Christian leaders, from House Speaker Mike Johnson (who describes the Bible as his worldview) to former evangelical congressional representative Stephen Fincher, justify cuts to food programs with verses like:[1]

- "If anyone is not willing to work, don't let him eat" (2 Thessalonians 3:10)
- "For you always have the poor with you" (Matthew 26:11)
- "But if anyone doesn't provide for his own … he has denied the faith and is worse than an unbeliever" (1 Timothy 5:8)
- "He who sows sparingly will also reap sparingly" (2 Corinthians 9:6)

---

1. Mike Johnson, "Interview on *The Sean Hannity Show*," Fox News, October 26, 2023; Rick Ungar, "GOP Congressman Stephen Fincher On A Mission From God—Starve The Poor While Personally Pocketing Millions In Farm Subsidies," Forbes, May 21, 2013, https://www.forbes.com/sites/rickungar/2013/05/22/gop-congressman-stephen-fincher-on-a-mission-from-god-starve-the-poor-while-personally-pocketing-millions-in-farm-subsidies/; see also Washington Post, "GOP lawmaker: The Bible says 'if a man will not work, he shall not eat'," March 30, 2017.

Tony Perkins (Family Research Council) and Robert Jeffress (First Baptist Dallas and presidential advisor) push to reduce government aid, saying that personal responsibility and local charity should replace "dependency" on government. True Christian compassion, they argue, teaches self-reliance and dignity. Handouts, they say, create lasting harm.

But here's a twist where private doubts sometimes slip through. Mary-Lou, the kitchen coordinator, argued for the pantry cuts but quietly packed boxes for two single dads, one of whom was an Iraq War veteran between shifts as a mechanic. "They're not freeloaders," she muttered, "they're just getting clobbered right now." Local conservative leaders rarely saw policy as simple, and at home, lines often blurred.

Even within these circles, some leaders worry that hard ideology is eclipsing compassion. Pastors warn that rigid stances risk blinding us to urgent needs.

THE PROGRESSIVE AND MAINLINE CHRISTIAN PERSPECTIVE

Shift the lens, and you'll see a very different definition of Christian responsibility to the hungry. Organizations such as Sojourners (Rev. Adam Russell Taylor), the Center on Faith and Justice (Jim Wallis), major denominations (United Methodist Church, Episcopal Church, Presbyterian Church U.S.A.), and Catholic Social Services advocate for robust aid, working directly with government to feed the hungry as a matter of faithful stewardship. They see cutting food assistance as betraying Gospel values.

Scriptural supports include:

- "I was hungry and you gave me food … because you did it to the least of these my brothers, you did it to me" (Matthew 25:35,40)

- "Isn't this the fast that I have chosen: to release the bonds of wickedness ... to distribute your bread to the hungry?" (Isaiah 58:6–7)

- "He who has pity on the poor lends to Yahweh" (Proverbs 19:17)

- "But whoever has the world's goods and sees his brother in need, then closes his heart ... how does God's love remain in him?" (1 John 3:17)

To these Christians, the Gospel demands systemic action. Jesus fed five thousand; no resumes required. The only test is whether we serve "the least of these"—no asterisks.

If we see a hungry child and call it "not the government's problem," it's no better than ignoring Jesus himself. Would anyone walk past a hungry Christ?

My view? If children are hungry, the Christian response isn't another lecture to parents. It's immediate, practical compassion. I once saw a progressive pastor lock arms with a conservative youth director to get free school breakfasts restored. "We can argue about budgets tomorrow," she said. "But this morning, nobody comes to class hungry."

THE HONEST DISAGREEMENT

Both camps appeal to Scripture. Both are sincere. Conservatives genuinely believe self-reliance honors dignity and guards against dependency. Progressives believe that compassion for hungry children is non-negotiable, and systemic issues require systemic remedies.

Real world: nearly 14 million American children face food

insecurity.[2] Most live in homes where someone is working. Two-thirds of aid goes to kids, seniors, or the disabled.[3] The core debate: Is Jesus served by local charity, or by collective action that can scale to millions? If you're still with me, you know why this matters for Emma, and for us.

PREFACE TO THE FOUR QUESTIONS

Before launching into the Four Questions, let's pause. The real work isn't about "winning" arguments, but moving closer to the life, character, and priorities of Jesus. These are not theological exam questions; they're what Jesus Himself used to measure faith: fruit that lasts, compassion that acts, empathy that transforms, and truth that frees.

Why These Questions?

The Jesus Principle isn't about scoring points in theological or political arguments, it's about honest, soul-searching discernment for believers and skeptics alike. In a world where Christians defend opposite policies, each "with the Bible in hand," we need more than proof-texts or slogans. The Four Questions cut through the noise and ask: Are we genuinely moving closer to the life, character, and priorities of Jesus, or are we simply reinforcing the boundaries of our own tribe?

1. Does This Bear the Fruit of the Spirit?

This question asks us to look at what our beliefs and choices actually produce in real life. Do they lead to actions and attitudes that

---

2. Child Hunger in America—Facts," Feeding America, last modified October 31, 2024, https://www.feedingamerica.org/hunger-in-america/child-hunger-facts.

3. United States Department of Agriculture, Economic Research Service, "Food Security in the U.S.—Key Statistics & Graphics," last updated July 31, 2025, http://www.ers.usda.gov/topics/food-nutrition-assistance/food-security-in-the-us/key-statistics-graphics.

reflect Christ's love, or do they result in outcomes that contradict His example? Born-again Christians are called to be transformed from the inside out by the Holy Spirit, which is a process that bears real, unmistakable fruit in everyday life. St. Paul's Galatians 5 lists "love, joy, peace, patience, kindness, goodness, faithfulness, gentleness, and self-control" as the actual evidence of the Spirit at work.

As the Spirit shapes us, these qualities arise and grow naturally, becoming more present the closer we draw to Jesus. But if what we believe and do produces the opposite—anger, division, fear, or strife—no matter how scriptural or righteous our arguments sound, something is off course. Christlikeness is never proven by doctrine alone, but by the qualities that flourish as the Holy Spirit truly transforms us. If the fruit isn't there—or it's bad fruit—it's a sign we may be moving in the wrong direction.

2. Does This Care for the Vulnerable: the Poor, the Marginalized, the Excluded?

Jesus's ministry centered on the "least of these"—the hungry, poor, sick, and oppressed—not just as a social cause but as the living embodiment of Himself. In Matthew 25, Jesus makes it unmistakably clear: "Whatever you do for the least of these, you do for me." That means every breakfast skipped, every child left hungry in school, every need unmet is as if it were happening to Jesus himself.

Would anyone leave an eight-year-old Jesus sitting at his desk in the morning with no food in his stomach and unable to concentrate on class? The consequences Jesus detailed aren't minor; he describes a horrendous fate for those who ignore or dismiss the least of these.

Compassion is not a suggestion for Christians; it's the defining measure of faith and a warning against religious self-deception. If a belief or policy leaves the vulnerable worse off, we are called to stop and reconsider, no matter how familiar or comfortable the alternative might be.

3. Would I Want This Done to Me, or to Those I Love?

This is the Golden Rule applied at every level of life, from lawmaking to family arguments. Jesus made it clear: "Do unto others as you would have them do unto you." He paired this with "love God" and taught that together, these two summed up all the Law and the Prophets, meaning, for Jesus, this simple principle is not just good advice, but the very heart of faithfulness.

When wrestling with difficult calls, this question flips the script from abstraction or rationalization to lived empathy. It asks, "If roles were reversed, would this action, law, or attitude feel just? Or would it feel like betrayal?" It's a safeguard against dehumanizing others and a summons to honesty and fairness in practice.

4. Is this true—aligned with the life and teaching of Jesus, and the facts?

Truth for Jesus wasn't just theological accuracy; it was lived integrity, a readiness to confront injustice and hypocrisy, even when costly or unpopular. This question demands self-examination about motives, facts, and consequences. It insists that sincerity and intensity are never substitutes for objective reality or Jesus-shaped honesty. If doctrine, policy, or tradition is revealed as false, performative, or inconsistent with Jesus's own life and words, this final question bids us to recalibrate, not retreat.

WHY THESE FOUR QUESTIONS? WHY NOW?

These questions are important because almost every schism in the church, every cultural crisis, and every failure of compassion can be traced to ignoring one or more of them. They're not about shaming or scoring, but about growing and drawing us back to the Jesus we claim, and challenging us to see if our faith is bearing His kind of fruit in a divided, hurting world.

Let these questions be your compass and filter. They won't give easy answers, but they'll always point in the direction of Christ.

THE JESUS PRINCIPLE AS COMPASS

The debates, pain, and confusion surrounding hunger and poverty can leave us disoriented. The Jesus Principle is a compass for those storms and not a shortcut or a party line, but a simple, repeated practice: *Is this thought, word, or action moving me toward Jesus—or away from him?*

This isn't a one-time verdict; it's daily calibration. Like checking true north, we ask it in ordinary moments: before we vote, post, spend, speak, or stay silent. Alone with God—no crowd, pastor, or friends to impress—we hold up each choice to the Jesus we meet in the Gospels.

When beliefs or instincts collide, we don't look for louder arguments; we look for alignment and direction. Are the vulnerable better cared for? Is mercy rising? Do we see the fruit of the Spirit? If not, the current is pulling us off course. Return to true north. Ask again. Keep asking. This is a meditation in motion, a continuum of awareness that forms a life.

THE JESUS PRINCIPLE AS FILTER

A compass is great for setting your direction, but even the clearest path can hide dangers you don't see coming. Imagine scooping water from a sparkling stream. It looks clean, maybe even tastes fresh. But before you drink it, you run it through a filter, because even the purest-looking water can carry invisible toxins that harm you from the inside out.

The Jesus Principle works the same way. It's not just a compass pointing you toward Christlike action. It's a filter for your beliefs, instincts, and traditions. Before you "drink in" a belief or pass it along, the Jesus Principle asks you to pause and run it through a deeper test of the four questions:

1. Is this consistent with the fruit of the Spirit? *(love, joy, peace, patience, kindness, goodness, faithfulness, gentleness, and self-control).*

> **CONSERVATIVE CHRISTIAN:** Let's get real. Endless free meals turn schools into feeding troughs, not launch pads. When kindness means coddling, we teach kids dependency, not dignity. Tough love means prepping kids for the real world, not endless handouts, so why pretend free lunch is the fruit of the Spirit?
>
> **PROGRESSIVE CHRISTIAN:** Denying breakfast and calling it tough love is moral malpractice because hungry kids don't learn; they just get left behind. Jesus didn't serve "self-reliance" at the table. He fed people, no questions asked. The only fruit you grow by gutting meal programs is shame, anxiety, and lost futures for kids who need hope most.

2. Does this care for the vulnerable: the poor, the sick, the marginalized, the excluded?

> **CONSERVATIVE CHRISTIAN:** Aid should go where it's truly desperate, not handed out like candy to everyone with their hand out. Accountability matters: free lunches and SNAP sound generous, but they can lock families into poverty cycles. Real care

lifts people up; it doesn't keep them stuck with government crutches.

PROGRESSIVE CHRISTIAN: The real damage comes when struggling kids are denied food; empty stomachs mean empty futures for those least able to bounce back. Cutting school meals punishes children for circumstances beyond their control, shaming the very people Jesus called us to protect. Justice isn't selective; either you feed hungry kids, or you don't.

3. Would I want this done to me or those I love?

CONSERVATIVE CHRISTIAN: Support should have real standards where dignity comes from breaking out of crisis, not settling into government reliance. No parent wants their child trapped in a cycle of handouts. Love means encouraging families to stand tall, not keeping people dependent out of misplaced compassion.

PROGRESSIVE CHRISTIAN: No one would tolerate hunger or cafeteria shame for a child they love. Kids deserve more than lectures. They need food in their bellies and a chance to thrive, every single day. The fruit of love is security, not rationed help or endless excuses.

4. Is this true—aligned with the life and teaching of Jesus, and the facts?

CONSERVATIVE CHRISTIAN: "Don't work, don't eat" isn't cruelty; it's a wake-up call to break cycles of need, not institutionalize them. Real help puts parents back in charge, not handcuffed to handouts. Setting standards isn't unloving; it's how families recover dignity and take pride in providing for their own.

Progressive Christian: Most kids going hungry have parents hustling, clocking low wages and unreliable hours, so this isn't about laziness; it's the math of poverty. Jesus fed the hungry without forms, tests, or caveats. Any policy that makes a starving kid prove their family "deserves" lunch is legalism dressed up as morality, and it misses the radical hospitality of Jesus.

WHAT TO FILTER OUT, WHAT TO KEEP?

Toss out:
- Policies that force deserving families out of programs for technicalities, paperwork failures, or minor income shifts
- Rhetoric about "dependency" that is used to eliminate or gut aid, when evidence shows hunger and trauma increase
- Theological arguments that justify hunger or shame recipients because the Gospels offer no defense for systems that inflict this kind of harm

Keep:
- Direct, unconditional food programs that measurably reduce child hunger and boost nutrition among the poor and vulnerable
- Safety nets that don't collapse over minor income changes or family structure: SNAP; Women, Infants, and Children (WIC); school lunches; and emergency pantries included
- Efforts/funding that prioritize feeding children, elders, disabled adults, and working poor before debates over "worthiness"

SUMMARY: PASS/FAIL FOR THE JESUS PRINCIPLE

In the end, the Jesus Principle filter is mercilessly revealing: If a church, government, or policy leaves more children going to bed hungry, it fails. If a decision sustains families, feeds the forgotten, and reflects the wild generosity of Jesus, it passes.

HISTORY'S HARD LESSONS

We've seen Christians use Scripture to defend slavery, segregation, exclusion, and even genocide. The church is replete with examples of Scripture bent to serve power, and of standards adjusted for political expedience (relative morality):

- The Southern Baptist Convention once supported abortion rights, then reversed its position for apparent political reasons.
- Many churches and denominations have apologized for covering up sexual abuse.
- Numerous evangelical churches once insisted on moral character for leaders, then moved the goalposts for political expedience.

Even well-intentioned believers can back systems of evil when dogma blinds them. The point isn't to shame, but to remind us that conviction, unchecked by compassion and discernment, leads to tragedy.

And this isn't just dusty history. The same patterns repeat today where beliefs seem rock-solid, right until they collide with real people's pain. Do we double down, or pause and look again for Jesus's face among those hurt?

THE STAKES TODAY

Dangerous patterns—like Christian nationalism—are rising again, now shaping laws, policy, and the American public square. Linked to movements like Project 2025, this brand of faith risks turning the Gospel into a tool of exclusion and harming vulnerable groups.

When faith becomes a weapon, the future of both church and democracy grows dim. If we don't reclaim the heart of Jesus now, we risk losing not just our spiritual foundation, but our hope for public life built on justice and mercy.

TEST DRIVE: THE JESUS PRINCIPLE

This isn't a new club, ritual, or hierarchy; it's a tool, quick to grab, easy to use. *Do your choices move you closer to Jesus—or away?*

In the next chapters, we'll run this filter through healthcare access, immigration, inequality, creation care, LGBTQ+ inclusion, Christian nationalism, and the role of women. We'll test every story and policy.

Don't worry about getting "right." The goal is honesty, not defense. If your belief doesn't pass, that's a place to grow, not retreat. The Jesus Principle is about direction and whether we are moving toward more mercy, justice, truth, and love, or clinging to comfort, habit, and tribe.

LOOKING AHEAD

Each chapter that follows is a new road test for faith. The Jesus Principle will be the compass and filter for real wounds, divides, and dilemmas. The answers won't always comfort—sometimes they sting.

But this is the work Jesus called us to: humble, truthful, unflinching. When the slogans fade and the noise quiets, only one question matters: Are we actually becoming more like Jesus?

Kyler's hand was easy to raise. His heart, though, is still searching the mirror, the same mirror awaiting each of us. Ready for the next turn? Emma is. The question is: are we?

CHAPTER 2

WOMEN AT THE CROSSROADS

WAITING ROOM OF HOPE AND FEAR

She sits in the hospital waiting room, her phone clutched tight, heart pounding out a rhythm only she can feel. Behind those double doors, her mother's life hangs in the balance—sepsis after a complicated birth—and the medical team has told her they have to wait until her mother is closer to death before they can act.

That's not a metaphor. That's the law in Texas now.

She's sixteen. Staring at her future reflected in glass: no comprehensive sex ed, birth control impossibly out of reach, and a culture where if a girl gets pregnant, she's left to fend for herself. No child support, no equal pay, no help for single mothers, and the boy who vanished isn't held responsible.

> Here, in this red state, being a girl means living at the crossroads of bravery and fear, and the uncertainty of which road she'll be forced to walk.
>
> Head bowed, she whispers a prayer. Can God help her mother when the state won't and the doctors can't?

Is this what it means to grow up Texan now, waiting, hoping, and wondering if this is all a young woman can expect: to be stuck on the edge, longing for compassion in a world run by policy and power?

What was once the rare, tragic drama of a single family is swiftly becoming the shared reality for women and girls in red states across America. What happens to one family in a Texas hospital today could be the fate of thousands tomorrow unless something changes.

WHEN THE LAW SAYS "WAIT UNTIL YOU'RE DYING"

Let's be honest: this is what happens when lawmakers, not doctors, sit in the driver's seat. Take Josseli Barnica: twenty-eight years old, thrilled to expand her family, and suddenly trapped in a nightmare. Her water breaks at seventeen weeks. Any basic OB textbook flags the danger: infection is coming fast. In nearly every blue state, doctors would intervene, protect Josseli, and give her a fighting chance.

Not in Texas.

Doctors looked at her, looked at the law, and told her to wait—for her fetus's heartbeat to stop, for infection to get worse, for some legal magic "moment" when they could act. Forty hours of dread.

Nothing. Her condition deteriorated. Dead, three days after birth; killed, not by chance, but by government policy.[4]

Amanda Zurawski's story? Practically a carbon copy. After her water breaks too soon, the hospital keeps her waiting, powerless, as infection takes root. By the time they can move, Amanda is in septic shock. She survives, but her body is forever changed, and her dreams for the future are haunted by the same policy that nearly killed her lost daughter Willow.[5]

Too dramatic? No. This isn't just an anecdote; this is the new operating manual in state after state. "There's nothing we can do, our hands are tied," goes the medical refrain. Why these laws? Why this cruelty? Because somewhere, a legislature full of mostly men decided that protecting a "heartbeat" on paper meant risking a breathing woman's life in practice.

Let's call it: when laws force doctors to gamble with women's lives, we aren't talking "pro-life." We're talking about a system that treats women's bodies as legal battlegrounds and medical professionals as enforcers of ideology, not agents of mercy.

If you think, "Surely this isn't the world our faith—or our country—set out to create," good. Because to get here, we must look at where we came from: not just the latest headline, but deep into the soil of American patriarchy, scriptural controversy, and the ancient urge to control women's destinies, all dressed up for a new century.

---

4. Kavitha Surana, "Josseli Barnica Died in Texas After Waiting 40 Hours for Miscarriage Care," ProPublica, October 29, 2024, https://www.propublica.org/article/josseli-barnica-death-miscarriage-texas-abortion-ban; Merck Manuals, "Prelabor Rupture of Membranes (PROM) - Gynecology and Obstetrics," updated April 10, 2024, https://www.merckmanuals.com/professional/gynecology-and-obstetrics/antenatal-complications/prelabor-rupture-of-membranes-prom.

5. Elizabeth Cohen, "Texas woman almost dies because she couldn't get an abortion," CNN, November 16, 2022, https://www.cnn.com/2022/11/16/health/abortion-texas-sepsis; Lauren McGaughy, "Amanda Zurawski, denied abortion in Texas, sues state after nearly dying," The Texas Tribune, July 18, 2023, https://www.texastribune.org/2023/07/19/texas-women-testify-abortion-ban/; Supreme Court of Texas, Zurawski v. State of Texas, 690 S.W.3d 644 (Tex. 2024).

PATRIARCHY THEN AND NOW: FROM BIBLE TO STATEHOUSE

Let's not sugarcoat it: America's laws and culture have always had patriarchy baked in. For generations, men wrote the rules—about women's bodies, property, work, and futures—and then dared to call it "biblical values." The roots aren't hard to find: Exodus 21:7–11 outright lists women as chattel, property to be bought and sold; Ephesians 5:22 has Paul instructing, "Wives, be subject to your own husbands, as to the Lord." For centuries, those verses forged shackles, which were often more than just metaphorical ones.

But don't confuse "in the Bible" with "blessed by Jesus." The Jesus in the Gospels broke the pattern. He counted Mary Magdalene among his true followers. He shielded the woman about to be stoned, flipping the whole crowd's sense of justice on its head: "He who is without sin among you, let him throw the first stone at her" (John 8:7). He let women's testimony anchor the resurrection story, which was a move so radical it scandalized every power structure of his day.

Fast-forward to now: Christian nationalism is busy drag-and-dropping Old Testament patriarchy right into American law, after announcing that it is Christ's will. Project 2025 isn't just legalese; it's a campaign to codify a selective, male-centered reading of scripture, rolling back hard-won freedoms and tightening state control over women's choices.[6]

Here's the shocking part: this isn't Saudi Arabia, it's the United States, land of the free, home of the mythically independent. Even

---

6. Carrie Baker, "The Next Battle for Equality," Smith Quarterly, February 17, 2025, https://www.smith.edu/news-events/news/next-battle-equality; Kettering Foundation, "Project 2025: The Blueprint for Christian Nationalist Regime Change," December 1, 2024, https://kettering.org/project-2025-the-blueprint-for-christian-nationalist-regime-change/; National Partnership for Women & Families, "Project 2025 Threatens Women and Families' Health and Freedom," March 5, 2025, https://nationalpartnership.org/report/project-2025-threatens-women-and-families-health-and-freedom/.

in Texas and Florida, where rugged individualism is on billboards and every pickup tailgate, people are cheering for a government that polices women's lives and reasserts male rule.

Ask yourself: whose rights does freedom protect if not everyone's? Authoritarianism always starts with the "other," but the net always widens. Today, it's women. Tomorrow, who's next?

If we're honest, these battles are as old as the republic, and the playbook is the same. Power writes rules. Justice bends. Suffering spreads out of sight until someone refuses to play along.

PROJECT 2025: THE WAR ON WOMEN'S FREEDOM

Here's where the quiet paperwork turns into a national crisis. Project 2025 is not just a think-tank fantasy: it's an extremist Christian nationalist blueprint backed by the Heritage Foundation, the Center for Renewing America, Turning Point USA, and more than a hundred conservative groups, aiming for nothing less than regime change by executive order. Page after page lays out a campaign to "make America biblical," but with a handpicked reading of scripture that privileges patriarchy and control.[7]

Let's spell out what that means for women. In Texas and Florida—the tip of the spear for national policy—the maternal mortality crisis has become a catastrophe. Texas posts one of the highest rates among developed nations, with Black women facing three times the risk of

---

7. National Partnership for Women & Families, "Project 2025 Threatens Women and Families' Health and Freedom," March 5, 2025, https://nationalpartnership.org/report/project-2025-threatens-women-and-families-health-and-freedom/; Carrie Baker, "The Next Battle for Equality," Smith Quarterly, February 17, 2025, https://www.smith.edu/news-events/news/next-battle-equality; Kettering Foundation, "Project 2025: The Blueprint for Christian Nationalist Regime Change," December 1, 2024, https://kettering.org/project-2025-the-blueprint-for-christian-nationalist-regime-change/.

dying in childbirth compared to white women.[8] Florida? Dead last for postpartum care, with nearly half of all maternal deaths happening after delivery, at the exact moment when Medicaid runs dry for new mothers.[9]

This isn't a statistical fluke. These are casualties racked up by deliberate policy choices: defunding public clinics, shuttering abortion access, rejecting federal Medicaid expansion, surveilling pregnancies, and criminalizing travel for care. Project 2025 would scale these playbooks federally: ban abortion with no exceptions—even for rape, incest, or medical risk—track and report pregnancy data and punish interstate travel by women seeking care. These aren't just restrictions. They're a wholesale erasure of personhood, turning women into state-owned property.

We're told, "It'll never happen here." Look again. Power doesn't rest when it has tasted blood. And while national debates bluster on cable news, data and stories from the front lines prove that these bans kill women, fracture families, and strip freedom from millions, all under the banner of Christian faith.

But here's the part that will make your blood boil: we already have proven answers.

TEEN PREGNANCY: A SOLVABLE CRISIS

Let headlines rage, but there are proven answers for cutting abortions and teen pregnancies. Colorado, for instance, cut teen births and abortions by over half with affordable contraception and honest sex education. Births to women without diplomas dropped, and public

---

8. Texas Maternal Mortality and Morbidity Review Committee and Department of State Health Services, "Joint Biennial Report 2024," August 31, 2024, https://www.dshs.texas.gov/sites/default/files/legislative/2024-Reports/MMMRC-DSHS-Joint-Biennial-Report–2024.pdf.

9. Florida Agency for Health Care Administration, "Maternal and Infant Mortality Report for Florida Medicaid," November 30, 2024, https://ahca.myflorida.com/content/download/25507/file/Maternal%20and%20Infant%20Mortality%20Report%202024.pdf.

assistance costs plunged. This isn't theory—it's real-world impact: when teens have knowledge and access, unplanned pregnancies and abortions fall. No culture war, just practical compassion.[10]

Contrast that with many red states, where abstinence-only programs prevail. The numbers show that teens still have sex—often more frequently—but are less likely to use protection, leading to more disease, more pregnancies, and more kids without support.[11] If prevention matters, why resist what works? Colorado's model respects teens' choices and reduces harm. Why wouldn't Texas and Florida follow suit? Is the goal well-being, or simply control? Or is it a practical case of religious dogma?

If so, let's just be honest. If the story conservatives tell themselves about abstinence-only sex ed doesn't match reality, maybe the real reason is simple: "We want to keep it because it's our religious conviction, good or bad, for better or worse." That's more honest than bending the facts to insist that abstinence-only education works best for young people when the evidence says otherwise.

It isn't just about sex ed. Programs providing confidential access and real support consistently drop pregnancy rates, but they're often axed for ideological reasons, not lack of results. The bigger picture? Policy fights sometimes aren't about stopping abortion; they're about preserving religious dogma at all costs, or keeping adult control, even at young people's expense.

Next up: theology. Both sides wield their Scripture, but what the Bible really says is far more nuanced, and much harder to pin down.

---

10. Colorado Department of Public Health and Environment, "Colorado's Success with Increasing Access to Long-Acting Reversible Contraception," January 2017, https://cdphe.colorado.gov/fpp/about-us/colorados-success-long-acting-reversible-contraception-larc.

11. Kathrin Stanger-Hall and David W. Hall, "Abstinence-Only Education and Teen Pregnancy Rates: Why We Need Comprehensive Sex Education in the U.S.," PLoS ONE 6, no. 10 (2011): e24658, https://pmc.ncbi.nlm.nih.gov/articles/PMC3194801/.

DUELING BIBLES: THE CONSERVATIVE CHRISTIAN PERSPECTIVE

For many conservative Christians, abortion isn't just about policy; it's a sacred issue, deeply entwined with Scripture and tradition. Organizations like Live Action (founded by Lila Rose), the Family Research Council (led by Tony Perkins), and Alliance Defending Freedom (with Kristen Waggoner at the helm), drive the anti-abortion movement's message. High-profile figures such as Abby Johnson have added personal testimony to the cause, portraying abortion as a fundamental moral evil to be fought at all costs.

Their scriptural foundation runs deep: "Before I formed you in the womb, I knew you. Before you were born, I sanctified you" (Jeremiah 1:5), and "For you formed my inmost being. You knit me together in my mother's womb ... I am fearfully and wonderfully made" (Psalm 139:13–16).

For this camp, life is seen as beginning at conception, and defending that life is viewed as a sacred duty. Some even oppose certain types of contraception and fertility treatments for all Americans, like IVF (*in vitro* fertilization), believing that any intervention in the natural process crosses a moral line.[12]

The impact of these policies is real and measurable. Since Texas severely restricted abortion access, maternal mortality rates jumped, especially for Black women, a trend that's not just a statistic, but a story told in emergency rooms and family heartbreak.[13]

When policies uphold "unborn life" but result in preventable deaths of mothers like Porsha Ngumezi (denied a standard D&C

---

12. Ruth Graham, "What Christian Traditions Say About I.V.F. Treatments," New York Times, February 25, 2024, https://www.nytimes.com/2024/02/24/us/christian-tradition-ivf.html.

13. Gender Equity Policy Institute, "Maternal Mortality in the United States After Abortion Bans," June 8, 2025, https://thegepi.org/maternal-mortality-abortion-bans/.

and ultimately lost to severe bleeding at home), shouldn't we pause? If saving the unborn is the goal, why aren't we as outraged by the death of women who could have been saved?

The tragedy in these stories isn't theoretical—it's direct, personal, and, too often, avoidable. For anyone insisting that the Bible's message is crystal clear, the real world keeps raising difficult questions. And on the other side, progressive Christians are asking their own questions, pointing to different verses, and to an equally deep moral well. Next, let's see what they're saying.

THE PROGRESSIVE AND MAINLINE CHRISTIAN APPROACH

Progressive and mainline Christians—like the Religious Coalition for Reproductive Choice (led by Rev. Katey Zeh), Catholics for Choice (with Jamie L. Manson), leaders like Union Theological Seminary's Rev. Serene Jones—read Scripture through a lens of justice, compassion, and agency. For them, reproductive rights tie directly to Christ's command to love and protect the vulnerable, defending each person's God-given autonomy.

Their biblical foundation differs from that of conservatives. Exodus 21 treats causing miscarriage as a fine, not murder, presenting a clear distinction between the life of a fetus and the life of a born person—and Numbers 5 appears to permit a ritual that induces miscarriage. Most critically, Jesus meets women with dignity, healing, and empowerment—as in the story of the hemorrhaging woman—restoring and blessing, not judging or controlling.

So for these Christians, the question shifts: "Are mothers protected? Are women able to choose freely, without shame or coercion?" The debate is less about biblical proof-texts and more about whose pain is recognized, whose agency is respected, and who is burdened by extra rules. They argue, justifiably, that Jesus sided with outsiders and refused to add burdens to the already weary.

As this struggle unfolds, one thing sharpens: theology is never just abstract. It shapes law, enforces silence, or sparks solidarity, and always determines who suffers, who thrives, and who gets heard.

WHERE ARE THE WHITE EVANGELICAL WOMEN?

If Christians are called to "serve justice to the poor and needy" (Proverbs 31:8–9), why does outrage over maternal mortality remain so quiet among white evangelical women? These women know the dangers of pregnancy and childbirth, yet as Black women in the South die at triple the rate of white women, evangelical moms rarely rally for change. Their quiet stands out next to decades of activism to restrict abortion in the name of "life."

For many conservatives, grief over abortion is real and rooted in faith. They mourn the loss of unborn souls, seeing every termination as a tragedy and the heartbreak is sincere. But why does this strong concern end at birth, instead of extending to mothers or the children facing hardship after delivery?

States with strict abortion bans also spend the least on maternal care, childcare, and paid leave.[14] Arkansas lawmakers even blocked attempts to extend Medicaid for new mothers, earning bipartisan criticism for hypocrisy.[15] Is the silence about political loyalty, racial bias,

---

14. Claire Cain Miller, "States With Abortion Bans Are Among Least Supportive for Mothers and Children," New York Times, July 28, 2022, https://www.nytimes.com/2022/07/28/upshot/abortion-bans-states-social-services.html.
15. Arkansas Advocates for Children and Families, "A Glaring Omission in Arkansas's Maternal Health Wins," June 26, 2025, https://www.aradvocates.org/a-glaring-omission-in-arkansass-maternal-health-wins/.

or simply not connecting law to real life? It's a challenge for every Christian, since Jesus broke barriers and lifted up the marginalized.

What if white evangelical women, who see themselves as guardians of life, championed both the unborn and mothers at risk? In the end, faith is measured not by words but by lives saved, voices heard, and justice done.

SPIRITUAL FREEDOM: A CHOICE BETWEEN AUTONOMY AND CONTROL

It's easy to lose sight, amid legal battles, that spiritual freedom isn't just political, but the heartbeat of faith. Real freedom means seeking God without fear or coercion. When laws or institutions enforce faith by decree, resentment—not reverence—follows.

Christian nationalism often touts "religious liberty" while passing laws that erase autonomy. Jesus taught, "Whatever you desire for men to do to you, you shall also do to them" (Matthew 7:12). If we wouldn't want our prayers or beliefs dictated, how can we justify stripping women's agency? Trying to "save" by force is not only legal overreach, but also a theological misunderstanding. Scripture is clear: "So then each one of us will give account of himself to God" (Romans 14:12).

Jesus never endorsed using state power to force faith or morality. He rebuked leaders who "bind heavy burdens ... but they ... will not lift a finger to help" (Matthew 23:4). The true promise of America and real faith is self-determination, even across disagreement. Threats to women's bodily autonomy are also threats to spiritual agency and moral relationship with God.

When faith is weaponized, it's not true piety. History proves that coercion never leads to lasting faith or genuine freedom.

THE JESUS PRINCIPLE AS A COMPASS

With faith, law, and morality so entangled, how do Christians (and communities) find an honest path forward? Here's where the Jesus Principle offers both a grounding compass and a pointed challenge. This principle asks us not to map every issue by party or doctrine but to hold up every law, policy, and private action to the simple question: "Does this belief or practice move you closer to the character and teachings of Jesus, or farther away?" The answer is between you and God.

It may help to ask yourself: Does coercion ever match the character or teachings of Jesus? Or is that drive to control ultimately a human impulse? What does the Spirit nudge—freedom or force? The truth may be revealed in the questions themselves.

THE JESUS PRINCIPLE AS A FILTER

A compass offers direction; a filter removes what is toxic before it can hurt us or others we offer it to. I offer four questions rooted in the character and teaching of Jesus and Paul to help us determine what to toss out and what to keep.

> **Warning:** What follows isn't a polite debate. It's the blunt, fire-breathing argument you'll actually hear from each corner. Guard your blood pressure.

1. Do your actions produce the fruit of the Spirit?

> **CONSERVATIVE CHRISTIAN:** If you claim to be Spirit-led, you protect life, from conception, no compromise. True love means telling hard truths, even if it stings. Killing the unborn poisons a nation's soul and mocks God's image in the womb. You want

fruit? Start by ending legalized death because anything less is rotting from the inside.

PROGRESSIVE CHRISTIAN: If your movement breeds fear, shame, and control, don't talk about spiritual "fruit"—call it what it is: toxic. Forcing birth while mothers die isn't love; it's cruelty dressed up as faith. Kindness? Gentleness? They show up in compassion for real women, not in policing their bodies through law and shame.

2. Does this care for the "least of these"?

CONSERVATIVE CHRISTIAN: The most vulnerable are the unborn—period. A civilized society draws the line at taking innocent life. Anything that makes abortion easier is abandoning the least of these. Real care is offering adoption and crisis pregnancy support, not murder in sterile rooms.

PROGRESSIVE CHRISTIAN: Vulnerability isn't just in the womb. It's the mother hemorrhaging in a Texas ER, the family bankrupted by forced birth, the child born into poverty or disability and then ignored. Care for the vulnerable? That's universal healthcare, real support, food, dignity, the stuff "pro-life" politicians keep slashing.

3. The Golden Rule: Would I want this forced on myself or those I love?

CONSERVATIVE CHRISTIAN: If truth offends, so be it. Righteous law demands sacrifice; smaller feelings don't trump eternal standards. If your family's comfort means legalizing murder, your moral compass is broken. Legislate what's right, not what's easy.

PROGRESSIVE CHRISTIAN: Picture your daughter, wife, or sister forced to beg for care or threatened with jail for crossing state lines for help. Would you want the state in your bedroom, your hospital room, your hardest nights? The Golden Rule: if you wouldn't wish it on your loved ones, don't vote it on strangers.

4. Is this aligned with truth as Jesus lived and taught it?

CONSERVATIVE CHRISTIAN: Jesus defended the innocent, even when it cost him friends and comfort. Scripture says, "Before I formed you in the womb, I knew you." There's no fudge room; God's law is higher than man's. Standing for life is standing for Christ, no matter who gets offended.

PROGRESSIVE CHRISTIAN: Jesus broke rules to heal, challenged power, and met women at their place of pain. If your "truth" leads you to ignore deaths, hunger, or trauma in the name of holiness, it isn't Jesus, it's just your brand of control. The real Christ put people before doctrine and always moved toward mercy.

THE JESUS PRINCIPLE AS A FILTER: WHAT TO TOSS, WHAT TO KEEP

The Jesus Principle means running every belief, policy, and "biblical" stance through a filter, not "Does this keep me comfortable?" but "Does this honor the dignity and agency of real people, especially women who bear the greatest cost?"

Toss out:

- Doctrines or policies that silence women in crisis or treat their agency as secondary

- Fear-driven laws that maintain predictable order for some while endangering others
- Filters that protect power, pride, or the security of the majority instead of the vulnerable
- The reflex to clamp down, control, and dictate, rooted more in anxiety than assurance

Keep:
- Humility that admits two Spirit-led Christians may see Scripture differently
- Courage to honor women's lived experience and agency, even when it complicates old certainties
- Filters that protect both women's conscience and their safety, and never one at the expense of the other
- Openness to letting go of convictions when they inflict harm instead of mercy
- Commitment to reducing abortions by proven means—like support for family planning, access to contraception, and holistic care for women and families—so that respect for life need not come at the cost of women's freedom or agency
- A willingness to fight for practical solutions, not just doctrinal victories, so fewer pregnancies end in abortion, and more mothers and children thrive

BOTTOM LINE

If the only way to preserve your filter is to control, silence, or dictate choices to others—instead of loving them through disagreement—it's time to reconsider. The only filter worth trusting is the one that lets women's voices, and their choices, truly pass through.

RECLAIMING FREEDOM AND MORAL AGENCY

Let's pause and look honestly at what's really at stake. At the heart of the Gospel is this one, fierce truth: each person stands alone before God, answering for their own soul, and no pastor, politician, or loved one gets to take that place. "Each one of us will give an account of himself to God" (Romans 14:12). That's the source of both our dignity and our responsibility. No one gets a free pass and no one else gets to rewrite that deal.

And yet, in today's America, women are too often treated as if they can't be trusted with their own choices. Laws and policies get rolled out as though a government office or church board knows better than a woman's own conscience. That's not faith; it's hubris dressed up as virtue. Let's name it: the urge to control, especially to control women, has more to do with old American myths of "chosenness" than anything Jesus ever taught.

"Chosenness" refers to the belief, rooted in American Puritan tradition, that the United States is uniquely favored or set apart by God for a special destiny or mission, a concept often invoked to justify moral or political control over others in the name of "divine purpose."

So when leaders thunder warnings of God's wrath for abortion, LGBTQ+ rights, or equality, they're not channeling the Gospel; they're playing out personal anxieties on the public stage, trying to command the weather with moral certainty. Still, let's be fair: protecting conscience doesn't mean free-for-all chaos. Societies need laws. But when law bulldozes agency or overrides conscience just to feel secure, both justice and the soul of the Gospel suffer.

Most Christians wrestle, honestly and humbly, with what faith demands. But some start with answers and grab for Scripture's proof-text just to win arguments. "Biblical values" become masks for fear and control, not the profound love at the center of Christ. This isn't some dry, academic debate. It's about who lives with the outcome, who carries the scars, and whose voice gets the last word in the most sacred space there is—the one between a person and God. That spot belongs wholly and forever to the individual. No spouse, pastor, lawmaker, or committee belongs there.

PERSUADE, DON'T COERCE

Here's the simplest test of our democracy: If abortion is to be banned, it should happen because hearts are persuaded, not because fists are clenched. That's the humility that democracy—and real faith—demand. No one's certainty should trample another's agency or conscience. Real freedom means majorities defend what's right, not just what's popular, especially when it's uncomfortable.

And yes, that standard works both ways, whether the fight is to defend access or to ban it outright. But in the end, the final say in your life isn't mine to give, and it isn't mine to take. That's the space reserved for you and for God alone.

History is plain: the moment anyone tries to close the door between a soul and God, well, that's the beginning of the end for both faith and freedom. Remember Roger Williams and those Baptists who preached "soul freedom." That spirit runs deeper than any law.

And let's not lose sight of the human reality behind this all: the girl in the waiting room whose future hangs in the balance, based not on her own voice, but on the decisions of strangers. Her birthright is agency. When history looks back, it won't just ask what laws were passed. It will ask: Who stood up, who stood by, and who remembered that agency was never anyone's to give, or to take away.

CHAPTER 3

HEALING OR HARM: THE COST OF SURVIVAL

He sits at the kitchen table. Bills spread like wounds across the grain, paystubs flanking hospital statements in uneven stacks. This is not the script anyone rehearsed: college degree, steady work, health insurance for the family.

By every rule of American adulthood, they are "responsible." They believed that by following the rules, they'd be protected.

But after his wife's diagnosis, every number on paper turns into a threat. Insurance, the supposed safety net, offers just a patchwork. Deductibles, co-pays, denied procedures—all blur together. The savings and 401k are gone, and the credit cards are maxed out. Even the children feel the tension as they watch corners being cut and note the silence about next month's groceries.

He drops his head into his hands. It's not defeat, but something deeper. Shame. A grief that survival now costs so much. He isn't praying for a miracle, just for someone to notice how this burden crushes his family.

He wonders if compassion still fits into policy or only comes after everything is lost.

THE COST OF GETTING SICK IN AMERICA

Getting sick in America is not just a health crisis. For many, it's an economic reckoning. The so-called "safety net" is a frayed rope ready to snap when it's needed the most, forcing responsible people to gamble with their lives.

Consider the numbers: as of 2022, nearly 27 million Americans were uninsured, which is more people than live in some entire countries.[16] Another 56 million are underinsured, left exposed to crushing bills despite carrying policies. Medical debt is a national plague with over half of adults struggling with it, and a quarter still repaying old bills. The total? At least $220 billion.[17] These figures show up in drained savings, wiped-out retirement accounts, skipped rent, skipped meals, and endless worry.

Personal stories slice deeper than statistics. Bob Ensor made headlines in 2018 when a sailboat accident sent him to an in-network

---

16. United States Census Bureau, "Health Insurance Coverage in the United States: 2022," last updated September 11, 2023, https://www.census.gov/library/publications/2023/demo/p60-281.html.

17. L. Levitt, "Medical Debt—The Canary in the Coal Mine for Health Care Affordability," JAMA Health Forum, September 5, 2024. https://jamanetwork.com/journals/jama-health-forum/fullarticle/2823514; KFF, "The Burden of Medical Debt in the United States," published August 8, 2025, https://www.kff.org/health-costs/the-burden-of-medical-debt-in-the-united-states/.

hospital. In a twist that should be impossible, his surgeons—unbeknownst to him—were out-of-network. His final bill: $167,000. Insurance shrugged; the rules allowed it.[18]

Most stories are kept quiet: families ration insulin, skip doctor visits, postpone treatment, wait for the crisis. Seven million Americans depend on insulin, but one in four admits they ration it because of cost.[19] For those lucky enough to be on Medicare or Medicaid, insulin caps offer relief. For millions with private insurance or no coverage, the fine print can mean life or death. Political debates erupt over whether to keep such price caps, as though the right to survive is up for review every session.

Medicaid is the backbone; nearly half of America's children rely on it for healthcare. It covers half of all births, sixty percent of nursing home stays, and 10 million people with disabilities.[20] Every year, politicians debate new requirements and spending cuts, putting millions at risk.

Economist Paul Krugman calls Medicaid "the last defense against bankruptcy" for 70 million Americans.[21] If lawmakers cut its funding or change eligibility, millions risk losing access to essential healthcare, financial stability, or even basic security.

---

18. Michelle Andrews, "How a Broken Nose from a Boating Accident Led to a $167,000 Plastic Surgery Bill," Kaiser Health News/ABC News, May 5, 2019, https://www.abcnews.go.com/Health/broken-nose-boating-accident-led-167000-plastic-surgery/story?id=62852530.

19. American Diabetes Association, "Insulin Cost & Affordability," updated April 30, 2024; CNN, "1.3 million Americans with diabetes rationed insulin in the past year," October 17, 2022.

20. American Hospital Association, "Fact Sheet: Medicaid," February 6, 2025, https://www.aha.org/fact-sheets/2025-02-07-fact-sheet-medicaid; KFF, "5 Key Facts About Medicaid and Pregnancy," August 10, 2025, https://www.kff.org/medicaid/5-key-facts-about-medicaid-and-pregnancy/; CDC, "Products - Data Briefs - Number 468 - May 2023," May 24, 2023, https://www.cdc.gov/nchs/products/databriefs/db468.htm.

21. Paul Krugman, "Republicans Beware: Medicaid Is Not a Soft Target," Paul Krugman Substack, July 1, 2025, https://paulkrugman.substack.com/p/republicans-beware-medicaid-is-not.

But this isn't just a budget line or talking point. Decisions made far away ripple through kitchens, churches, and grocery aisles. Security and vulnerability have nearly become synonyms. Every year, tens of thousands lose their footing because they simply can't afford care. Despite spending more per person than any other wealthy country, the U.S. falls behind in outcomes.[22]

The unavoidable question remains: What does it say about us, as a country, that even those who do everything "right" are one illness away from the edge?

DUELING BIBLES: MORAL DIVIDE AMONG CHRISTIANS

American Christians do not speak with one voice on healthcare. With so much on the line—health, dignity, solvency—one might expect believers, grounded in the same Gospel, to unite around solutions. Instead, reality is messier. Family tables, church sanctuaries, and policy organizations become arenas for conflicting answers, each camp sure they're defending biblical principles.

THE CONSERVATIVE CHRISTIAN PERSPECTIVE

Many conservative Christians, including leaders like Tony Perkins of the Family Research Council, resist government-led healthcare not from indifference, but out of biblical conviction. The refrain is clear: "But if anyone doesn't provide for his own, and especially his own household, he has denied the faith and is worse than an

---

22. Peterson-KFF Health System Tracker, "How does health spending in the U.S. compare to other countries?," updated April 8, 2025, https://www.healthsystemtracker.org/chart-collection/health-spending-u-s-compare-countries/; Commonwealth Fund, "US Health Care System Ranks Last Overall Among Other High-Income Countries," September 26, 2025, https://www.ajmc.com/view/us-health-care-system-ranks-last-overall-among-other-high-income-countries.

unbeliever" (1 Timothy 5:8). This is doctrine heard in small towns and church foyers.

Another foundation: "If anyone is not willing to work, don't let him eat" (2 Thessalonians 3:10). For this group, values like hard work and self-reliance are not American inventions but acts of faith. Eric Scheidler and the Stand Up for Religious Freedom Coalition defend conscience rights and warn about state intrusion on deeply held beliefs.

In practice, charity is personal and local. Skepticism about Medicaid or the Affordable Care Act is fierce. They worry these programs breed bureaucracy, dependency, and inefficiency. Proverbs echoes: "The soul of the sluggard desires, and has nothing, but the desire of the diligent shall be fully satisfied" (Proverbs 13:4).

Critics may see this as stingy, but for most, it's mercy channeled into hands-on solutions. More church outreach, less bureaucracy; sleeves rolled up, compassion delivered in person.

THE PROGRESSIVE AND MAINLINE CHRISTIAN PERSPECTIVE

Move across the aisle and another vision emerges. Progressive and mainline Christians, from Rev. Raphael Warnock (senior pastor of Atlanta's Ebenezer Baptist Church and U.S. senator) to Traci Blackmon (former Senior Pastor at Christ the King United Church of Christ in Missouri), insist that following Jesus means collective responsibility, especially for the vulnerable. Psalm 82 shouts: "Defend the weak, the poor, and the fatherless ... Rescue the weak and needy."

The Epistle of James goes further: "If a brother or sister is naked and lacks daily food, and one of you tells them, 'Go in peace. Be warmed and filled;' yet you didn't give them the things the body needs, what good is it? Even so, faith, if it has no works, is dead in itself" (James 2:15–17).

The Good Samaritan didn't just pray; he paid the bill. Blackmon calls healthcare a test of neighbor-love and justice. For many, letting millions fall through the cracks is not just failure; it's sin, a betrayal of Christ's heart. The call is for love of neighbor to show up in budgets and laws, not just worship.

Advocates highlight economic truth: nearly two-thirds of America's uninsured are working, often multiple jobs, yet are locked out by cost or circumstance.[23] Cuts to Medicaid could mean 50,000 preventable deaths.[24] Policy failure is a moral disaster.

In the pews, policy forums, and hospital rooms, these rival Bibles clash and mix, each chasing Christ's heart for the hurting.

THE JESUS PRINCIPLE AS A COMPASS

"True north" isn't left or right, but a lived direction, a trajectory pointed squarely at the teachings of Christ. Are policies, budgets, and daily choices inching toward sacrificial love, honesty, and the courage to bear one another's burdens (Galatians 6:2)? Are the poor actually cared for? If not—why not, really?

This isn't about impressing a preacher, winning an argument, or scoring points for a party. The only audience here is you and God, alone at the end of the day. In that quiet, honest space, ask yourself: are these choices—public and private—really moving me, my community, my nation closer to the heart of Jesus, or making excuses for drifting away?

---

23. Kaiser Family Foundation, "Key Facts about the Uninsured Population," August 8, 2025, https://www.kff.org/uninsured/key-facts-about-the-uninsured-population/.

24. Yale School of Public Health, "Proposed Federal Budget Could Lead to Over 51,000 Preventable Deaths, Researchers Warn in Letter to Senate Leaders," March 5, 2025, https://ysph.yale.edu/news-article/proposed-federal-budget-could-lead-to-over-51000-preventable-deaths-researchers-warn-in-letter-to-senate-leaders/.

Let that question—not anyone's approval—be your compass.

THE JESUS PRINCIPLE AS A FILTER

A compass sets the direction, but the filter tests every step for purity. Here, four hard-edged questions cut away pretense:

1. Is this consistent with the fruit of the Spirit?

CONSERVATIVE CHRISTIAN: True compassion means responsible care, not endless government bailouts. Blind handouts distort dignity. If society shields everyone from cost, who will value health? Private charity, not bureaucratic programs, delivers real help, otherwise you risk dependency, waste, and moral decay. In healthcare, nothing free is truly valued.

PROGRESSIVE CHRISTIAN: If a healthcare policy lets 50,000 Americans die every year from lack of coverage, rationing insulin, or skipping doctor visits because of price, that isn't love—it's neglect. The Spirit's fruit shows up in full stomachs, medicine bottles, and parents who sleep at night knowing their diabetic kid won't die early. Cruel systems create unnecessary suffering; Jesus would call it out, not explain it away.

2. Does this care for the vulnerable?

CONSERVATIVE CHRISTIAN: Genuine care lifts people out of long-term dependency. Medicaid and Medicare are lifelines, yes, but the routine expansion of benefits without cost controls lets expenses spiral, threatening solvency for all. People need help, but don't create a system that encourages people to stay sick or unemployed to qualify. Tough requirements are sometimes the only way to guarantee funds for future generations.

Progressive Christian: Paperwork hurdles, insurance denials, and tough love rules kill people. There's nothing accountable about denying medicine or cancer treatment because a kid's family missed paperwork by a month or earned a few dollars too much. The vulnerable—disabled, poor, elderly—don't need tests, they need actual care. Jesus gravitated to the margins; systems that leave them there betray Him and us.

3. Would I want this done to me or someone I love?

Conservative Christian: If I lost my job or got cancer, I'd want a hand, but also a path to getting back on my feet. Free rides and open wallets build dependence. If government insurance covers everything, people may game the system, leaving less for those who truly need it later. Give enough to restore; don't smother with "compassion" that leaves people stuck.

Progressive Christian: If your own child's future depended on a bureaucratic maze, high deductibles, and leftover policy scraps, you'd fight for more. Would you accept your parent dying younger because preventive care was unaffordable? Would you let your grandchild's school fundraiser pay for her leukemia treatment, just because she was born in the wrong state? Play out the Golden Rule in real time, would you tolerate these odds for yourself?

4. Does this align with truth as Jesus lived and taught it?

Conservative Christian: Jesus's parables respected the need for stewardship, for a system that runs on infinite benefits soon runs aground. The Bible warns about the sluggard and praises the diligent provider. Policies must mask mercy with discipline, or they risk enabling irresponsibility. Remove incentives to misuse the system, or everyone pays the price.

PROGRESSIVE CHRISTIAN: Jesus never asked for co-pays or insurance cards. He didn't withhold healing as leverage or punish the sick to teach a lesson. He spent His anger on religious profiteers and His compassion on the sick. The truth? Systems built on profit, exclusion, and endless hurdles for the needy would have triggered table-flipping, not approval.

WHAT TO TOSS, WHAT TO KEEP

When the Jesus Principle filter is applied to American healthcare, the results are blunt. Some policies, practices, and arguments clearly belong; others must be swept away, no matter how long they've lingered.

Toss out:
- Coverage cliffs, loopholes, eligibility landmines, or means-testing that makes healthcare a moving target. If a person is rejected for earning a dollar too much or living in the wrong county, that policy flunks.

- Work requirements, punitive rules, and bureaucratic hoops that force the sick and needy off the safety net while pretending to save money.

- Any plan that keeps profits high by squeezing coverage, hiking prices, or excluding whole categories of Americans.

- Arguments and legislation that tolerate tens of thousands of preventable deaths, normalized bankruptcies, or systematic neglect of the vulnerable.

- Politicized rhetoric that pretends health is a luxury or afterthought: ignore it. Health coverage is the bedrock of justice, security, and possibility for families and communities.

Keep:

- Any law or funding that cuts preventable deaths, extends coverage, and puts medicine and doctors within reach for everyone, not just the lucky.

- Reforms that guarantee preventive care: easier screenings, vaccines, timely treatment, and mental health as part of the basics.

- Systems and insurance models that refuse to leave anyone behind for lack of money, paperwork, or bad timing, especially children, elders, the disabled, and families working two jobs.

- Innovations that shrink the paperwork jungle and get lifesaving medicine and urgent care to those living paycheck to paycheck.

- Policies with proven track records: longer life expectancy, lower bankruptcy rates, less skipped care, and generational opportunity, not just bare survival.

FILTER SUMMARY: PASS/FAIL

The Jesus Principle filter doesn't respect party lines, conventional wisdom, or wishful thinking. It discards any system that leaves people out, delays care, or trades health for profit or "discipline." It keeps what saves lives, lowers barriers, honors dignity, and echoes Christ's standard for justice. The only question that matters: would you trust your family's future to this system? If not, it flunks. If yes, fight for it—your neighbor's life may depend on it.

A JESUS-CENTERED VISION

What would a healthcare system shaped by Jesus look like? Not like today's maze of coverage, co-pays, and out-of-pocket chaos. It would flip the script: prevention before profit, dignity before numbers, justice before convenience. Healing would be a promise, not a privilege.

History shows us the early church-built hospitals, monasteries, caring for the unwanted, the poor, the dying.[25] Modern clinics like Culture of Life Ministries (Texas, conservative model) or Christ Health Center (Alabama, centrist) provide whole-person care, treating people as neighbors rather than numbers.

Such a system would mean:

- *Solidarity*: The community carries each other's burdens.
- *Subsidiarity*: Local, faith-based solutions matter, but when the burden overwhelms, state and national safety nets must step up.
- *Dignity*: Every patient is seen, known, respected, and never just a case file.
- *Justice*: Policies are measured by their effects on those at the margins.

Medicare protects millions of our seniors from poverty. What could

---

25. Gary B. Ferngren, "Medicine and Health Care in Early Christianity," Johns Hopkins University Press, 2009; Christian History Institute, "From Poorhouse to Hospital," Christian History Magazine, accessed September 27, 2025, https://christianhistoryinstitute.org/magazine/article/from-poorhouse-to-hospital.

universal coverage do for children, working families, or the disabled? Galatians 6:2 commands: "Carry each other's burdens."

This isn't about red vs. blue, but the balance between prosperity and responsibility. Profits and stocks power our wealth, but mercy and mutual aid preserve our character.

BOTTOM LINE

More than 25 million Americans remain uninsured.[26] Even more are insured in name only. Lives are shortened, suffering needlessly multiplied, and the soul of the nation eroded by endless compromise. Both left and right claim victory, but talk is cheap. The test is real: do lives improve, do burdens lessen, do vulnerable people get what Jesus would demand?

A Christian not chained to party or program knows: the litmus test isn't who wins, but whether the least are served. If coverage leaves anyone out, we press on. National programs, local care, innovation—whatever works, we back it until the job is done.

The man at the kitchen table, searching for mercy, deserves better than slogans. So does the uninsured mother who must choose between groceries and insulin. So do you. So do we all.

If the system leaves anyone out, our work—and our witness—is unfinished.

---

26. Kaiser Family Foundation, "Key Facts about the Uninsured Population," August 8, 2025, https://www.kff.org/uninsured/key-facts-about-the-uninsured-population/; CDC, "Health Insurance Coverage: Early Release of Estimates from the National Health Interview Survey, 2024," June 24, 2025, https://www.cdc.gov/nchs/pressroom/releases/20250624.html.

CHAPTER 4

JUSTICE FOR ALL

JAMAL'S MORNING: TWO WORLDS, ONE DREAM

Jamal wakes up before sunrise to the rattle of the heating pipes and the distant thump of neighbors on the stairs. The apartment smells faintly of fried onions and floor cleaner as last night's dinner clings to the air.

His mother is already gone, stocking shelves at dawn, driving rideshare by midday, and cleaning offices late into the night.

He pours cereal alone at the chipped kitchen table, listening to the radio mumble headlines about school budgets and bus delays. At school, Jamal sees peeling paint, crowded classrooms, and textbooks older than he is; the rubber floor tiles squeak under worn-out sneakers.

When Jamal asks about honors classes, his counselor tells him, "Focus on staying out of trouble."

At home, his mom reminds him that education is the way forward. Yet Jamal can't help but notice that the doors always seem heavier for families like his.

If America believes in equal opportunity, why do the rules feel so different for kids that look like him?

WHY THIS CHAPTER WEAVES THREE THREADS

Let's be honest. For Jamal and millions like him, the story doesn't start with economics—it starts with race. Race shapes which neighborhoods families live in, which schools their kids attend, and which doors seem closed before anyone even gets a fair turn at the knob. Education doesn't break the cycle on its own; it often tightens the lock.

Schools in those neighborhoods are short on resources and overloaded with challenges: underfunded classrooms, outdated materials, and a system rigged so fewer kids make it to advanced courses or graduation day. But that's not just about education, it's about an architecture that's been designed, over generations, to favor some and hold back others.

When education falls short, opportunity shrinks. The result? Lower pay. Empty savings. Dreams sorted by skin color and street address. Race and education, woven together, fuel inequality regarding who gets ahead and who gets left behind. That's no accident, and it's not bad luck. It's the system at work.

THE JESUS PRINCIPLE AND AMERICA'S ORIGINAL SIN

Jamal's question—why does America promise equal opportunity but deliver two separate worlds?—strikes at the very heart of the Jesus

Principle. If faith is measured by how we treat the vulnerable, what does it say about a country where a child's destiny hangs on their address, the color of their skin, or the size of their parents' paycheck?

America's story is full of contradiction: "liberty and justice for all" on one hand, but in practice, race, class, and education have always shaped who gets a fair shot. During slavery, Black Americans were forbidden by law from learning to read. Long after slavery, barriers to education—segregated schools, redlined neighborhoods, biased testing—kept opportunity out of reach for Black families and other people of color. Today, underfunded schools in low-income communities remain the norm, not the exception, for many students of color.

The numbers tell the story: the median wealth of white families is more than ten times that of Black families, a gap reflecting generations of stolen chances and locked doors.[27] Even among college-educated families, Black and Hispanic households still face structural barriers to building wealth, securing housing, and accessing care.[28] Disparities in school discipline, testing, and placement in advanced classes serve to widen the achievement gap, making the ladder lean steeper and the climb even tougher.[29]

Modern tactics are more subtle but just as effective: gerrymandered voting districts, restrictive election laws, and systematic underfunding of public education keep marginalized communities voiceless and starved

---

27. U.S. Census Bureau, "Wealth by Race of Householder," April 22, 2024, https://www.census.gov/library/stories/2024/04/wealth-by-race.html.

28. Duke University, "U.S. Racial Wealth Gap Is Persistent And Growing, New Research Finds," June 9, 2024, https://news.duke.edu/stories/2024/06/10/u-s-racial-wealth-gap-is-persistent-and-growing-new-research-finds/.

29. Francis Pearman, "Racial disparities in school discipline are linked to the achievement gap between Black and white students," Stanford Graduate School of Education, September 24, 2025, https://ed.stanford.edu/news/racial-disparities-school-discipline-are-linked-achievement-gap-between-black-and-white.

of resources.[30] Racism isn't a footnote in America's story of economic inequality, it's the first chapter, and the thread running through every page.

THE MANAGED AMERICAN DREAM: HOW POLICY CREATED INEQUALITY

Let's say this out loud: America isn't really a free market paradise. It's a managed system—micromanaged, really—by policies cooked up in city halls, state capitals, and Congress. For four decades and counting, those policies have lined the pockets of corporations, CEOs, and the richest citizens, funneling opportunity up rather than out.

The big pivot came in the Reagan era, with "trickle-down economics." The pitch was simple: Cut taxes for the wealthy, and prosperity will float down to everyone else. But here's the truth: prosperity didn't trickle. It pooled. CEO pay went wild, unions were gutted, and wage growth flatlined for the families that needed it most. Meanwhile, corporate profits and stock markets soared.

The facts? Instead of having a strong middle class, like we did before Reagan, over sixty percent of Americans now live paycheck to paycheck, and nearly four in ten can't cover a $400 emergency without going into debt.[31] One surprise expense—one busted transmission or ER visit—can tip a family into crisis. But this isn't chance. It's the result of policy. If laws can funnel wealth upward, they can unlock opportunity downward just as fast.

Here's the real kicker: Not all Americans are hurt equally. Black, Hispanic, and Indigenous families face steeper odds, including higher

---

30. Brennan Center for Justice, "Voting Laws Roundup: 2024," May 31, 2024, https://www.brennancenter.org/our-work/research-reports/voting-laws-roundup-2024.
31. Federal Reserve Board, "Report on the Economic Well-Being of U.S. Households in 2024," June 11, 2025, https://www.federalreserve.gov/publications/2025-economic-well-being-of-us-households-in-2024-savings-and-investments.htm.

unemployment, lower wages, and tougher hurdles to homeownership. Old practices like redlining and new tricks like predatory lending keep the racial wealth gap stubbornly wide, making security and stability harder to reach for families of color. The system isn't broken; it's ordered to work this way.[32]

Redlining is the discriminatory practice of denying loans or services to people in certain neighborhoods—mainly communities of color—based solely on where they live, not their individual credit or qualifications. Predatory lending is the practice of imposing unfair, deceptive, or abusive loan terms—often with high fees or interest rates—on vulnerable borrowers, trapping them in debt and financial hardship.

EDUCATION AND INEQUALITY: THE ENGINE OF OPPORTUNITY, DERAILED

Nowhere is the impact of inequality clearer than in America's schools. The promise? Education should be the great equalizer, a ladder out, for any kid willing to climb. The reality? In this country, a child's education is mostly determined by their ZIP code and the color of their skin.

Underfunded public schools in poor neighborhoods mean crowded classrooms, outdated books, and overwhelmed teachers. Kids who start behind? Most never catch up. Programs like vouchers, which claim to offer "school choice," often move resources from public schools to private ones that can exclude disabled kids, LGBTQ+ students, and anyone who doesn't fit their mold.[33]

---

32. RootsofWealth Research Team, "Roots of Wealth: Racial Wealth Gap Barriers," Kindred Futures, August 25, 2025, https://kindredfutures.org/wp-content/uploads/2025/08/RootsofWealth-R4.pdf.

33. Wisconsin Watch, "Voucher schools discriminate against LGBTQ+, disabilities," November 26, 2023, https://wisconsinwatch.org/2023/05/wisconsin-voucher-schools-discrimination-lgbtq-disabilities/.

Racial inequality shows up everywhere, not just in money, but in daily experience. Black students are more likely to face suspension for the same behaviors as their white peers, and less likely to land in advanced classes.[34] Curriculum too often skips the contributions and struggles of people of color, reinforcing the message: some histories matter, others don't.

For half a century, conservative Christians have worked to gut the Department of Education, painting it as an overreach. But here's what the Department actually does: it protects civil rights, supports the most under-resourced districts, guarantees education for disabled students, and runs the federal student aid programs that give millions a shot at college. In short, it tries to keep doors open for the kids who need them most.[35]

All of this is at risk. A powerful coalition, including conservative Christian activists, is pushing to erase federal protections and oversight. The drive to remake public education around a narrow religious agenda has been building for decades and now stands closer to reality than ever. If that vision wins, who decides which faith gets taught, which books get banned, and whose version of history becomes "truth"? These are battles that decide more than curriculum—they decide whose future counts.[36]

---

34. Sean Darling-Hammond & Eric Ho, "No Matter How You Slice It, Black Students Are Punished More," American Educational Research Association Open, November 11, 2024, https://journals.sagepub.com/doi/full/10.1177/23328584241293411.

35. Urban Institute, "How Dismantling the Education Department Could Affect Disabled Students Across the US," February 18, 2025, https://www.urban.org/urban-wire/how-dismantling-education-department-could-affect-disabled-students-across-us.

36. Education Week, "Christianity Is Ramping Up in Public Schools. Where Is This Headed?" June 18, 2025, https://www.edweek.org/policy-politics/christianity-is-ramping-up-in-public-schools-where-is-this-headed/2025/06.

WHITEWASHING HISTORY AND THE ATTACK ON DEI: WHO BENEFITS?

Inequality in education isn't just about money. It's also about whose stories get told, which truths get aired, and which voices get silenced in the classroom. From coast to coast, a new front in the culture wars is raging inside America's schools, a systematic erasure of uncomfortable facts and marginalized perspectives, all under the flag of "protecting tradition."

Christian nationalism and its allies are working overtime: whitewashing history, banning books, and attacking diversity, equity, and inclusion (DEI) initiatives.[37] But what is DEI, really?

- Diversity: Different backgrounds at the table.
- Equity: Fair chances for everyone, not just the lucky few.
- Inclusion: Every voice counts; nobody left out or pushed aside.

When schools ban books by Black authors or erase the lessons of slavery and civil rights, they send a message: some stories, some struggles, are disposable. This isn't only about history, it's about whether every kid finds their own story in the textbook, or disappears completely.

Absurd bans keep piling up. Shel Silverstein's *The Giving Tree*—a gentle picture book—has landed on no-read lists for "promoting unhealthy relationships" or "environmental exploitation." If even *The Giving Tree* is suspect, what hope is there for honest conversations about race, justice, or American identity?[38]

---

37. Interfaith Alliance, "Anti-Censorship - Education Not Indoctrination," August 15, 2025, https://interfaithalliance.org/issues/anti-censorship.

38. Brittany L. Davis, "Brittany's Book Corner—Banned Books: 'The Giving Tree,'" Tropolitan, October 2, 2024, https://www.tropnews.com/post/brittany-s-book-corner-6.

The U.S. Naval Academy recently pulled Maya Angelou's *I Know Why the Caged Bird Sings* and other DEI-focused books from its shelves, while keeping Adolf Hitler's *Mein Kampf*.[39] Not an accident. Not a one-off. It was a decision by military leadership, a signal that books challenging white Christian America are unwelcome, while the tools of hate and exclusion remain accessible.

So, who wins when DEI gets gutted and history is whitewashed? Not the students, not struggling families, just the few desperate to keep the old pecking order intact. Here's the twist: Defending DEI isn't merely a partisan project. It's about faithfulness. For Christians, DEI aren't borrowed from partisan playbooks, they're rooted in the story of creation and the ministry of Jesus. Scripture shows God's passion for a vibrant, diverse humanity, united but not uniform, and repeatedly calls for justice, fairness, and mercy for the marginalized.

Jesus didn't just debate uncomfortable truths. He lived them, crossed social and religious boundaries, and lifted up those pushed to the margins. Welcoming outsiders, calling out hypocrisy, championing the vulnerable: that wasn't "activism," it was, and is, the core of the Gospel.

Defending honest history isn't politics. It's following Jesus's example and making room for every kid at the table.

LEGAL CORRUPTION: LOBBYING AGAINST THE POOR

Let's talk about who actually gets a seat at the table when laws are written in America. Too often, it's not Jamal's family, or anyone hustling through low-wage jobs or hoping for a break. Lobbying—supposedly

---

39. New York Times, "Who's In and Who's Out at the Naval Academy's Library?," April 11, 2025, https://www.nytimes.com/2025/04/11/us/politics/naval-academy-banned-books.html.

just "advocacy"—has turned into big business. Billion-dollar corporations and ultra-wealthy individuals spend lavishly to craft laws that pad their profits and chip away at protections meant for everyone else.

Take the Consumer Financial Protection Bureau (CFPB), born after the 2008 financial crisis to keep Americans safe from predatory lending and financial abuse. Banks and lenders spent fortunes lobbying to gut its power. The result? When the Trump administration moved to cut the CFPB's funding and oversight, it wasn't a fluke, it was the logical outcome of years of relentless, big-money advocacy.

Senator Elizabeth Warren and the original watchdogs at the CFPB returned nearly $20 billion to consumers through enforcement actions. When those protections are weakened, millions of everyday Americans become easy prey for the most powerful players on Wall Street.[40]

And it doesn't stop at banks. Companies as big as Walmart spend millions to oppose minimum wage hikes, even when their workers rely on food stamps and Medicaid just to feed their families and see a doctor, while the Walton family, now worth over $240 billion, collects the profits.[41]

Supporters of low minimum wages argue that keeping wages down allows businesses to create or preserve more jobs, claiming that raising pay leads to higher costs and fewer opportunities for workers, especially those just starting out.[42] But why should taxpayers subsi-

---

40. Consumer Financial Protection Bureau, "CFPB by the Numbers," April 2025, https://www.consumerfinance.gov/about-us/blog/cfpb-by-the-numbers/.
41. Los Angeles Times, "Who profits most from Medicaid and food stamps? Big, low-wage employers like Walmart and Amazon," July 1, 2025, https://www.latimes.com/business/story/2025-07-01/who-profits-most-from-medicaid-and-food-stamps-big-low-wage-employers-like-walmart-and-amazon.
42. Economic Policy Institute, "Raising the federal minimum wage to $15 by 2025 would lift the pay of 32 million workers," March 8, 2021, https://www.epi.org/publication/raising-the-federal-minimum-wage-to-15-by-2025-would-lift-the-pay-of-32-million-workers/.

dize poverty wages just so a handful of billionaires can add another zero to their bank accounts?

Meanwhile, school voucher schemes and efforts to privatize education are made possible by well-funded lobbies—including private school associations and conservative Christian groups—who invest millions to swing laws in their favor, usually at the expense of the public good.[43]

The poor don't have lobbyists. Sometimes, Christians with power use their faith to guard privilege instead of lifting up the vulnerable (see Proverbs 31:8–9). I don't think that's what Jesus meant for us to do.

THE PROSPERITY GOSPEL: GREED WITH A HALO

Now let's talk about a uniquely American distortion: the prosperity gospel. This theology claims wealth signals God's special favor, while poverty is treated as a sign of spiritual failure. That idea didn't drift down from the Sermon on the Mount; it exploded out of a twentieth-century marriage between American consumerism and religious fervor.[44]

Prosperity preachers—from Russell Conwell and E. W. Kenyon, to Oral Roberts, Kenneth Copeland, Benny Hinn, Joel Osteen, Paula White, and Creflo Dollar—taught millions that "sowing a seed" (usually a donation to their ministries) would unlock blessings and miracles. The theory goes: Believe hard, give big, get rich. But in real life,

---

43. First Focus, "School Vouchers and the growing threat to public education," January 30, 2025, https://firstfocus.org/resource/school-vouchers-issue-brief/.

44. White Paper: The Negative Effects of the Prosperity Gospel on Those Who Fail to Prosper, August 24, 2025, https://edgeinducedcohesion.blog/2025/08/25/white-paper-the-negative-effects-of-the-prosperity-gospel-on-those-who-fail-to-prosper/.The Gospel Coalition, "Prosperity Gospel Born in the USA," November 14, 2018, https://www.thegospelcoalition.org/article/prosperity-gospel-born-in-the-usa/.

it's often the preachers who strike it rich, while the poor and sick are blamed for lacking faith or generosity.[45]

The sad irony is that this gospel takes root not in the life of Jesus, but in the hyper-individualism and excess of American capitalism. Traditional Christian teaching called for sacrifice, justice, and care for the poor. But the prosperity gospel reframes greed as "faith," and situational morality as "God's blessing." Extravagance is treated as devotion.

The consequences? Instead of inspiring service and generosity to the "least of these," followers are told poverty and suffering are personal failings. Every struggle becomes a verdict: If you're struggling, pray harder and give more. This cycle enriches pastors but leaves many believers desperate and ashamed when miracles don't arrive.[46]

And yet, when disaster struck—think Hurricane Harvey pummeling Houston—the spotlight didn't just shine on everyday heroes like Jim "Mattress Mack" McIngvale, who opened his furniture stores immediately and sent trucks to rescue evacuees. It turned quickly to prosperity preacher, Joel Osteen, and Lakewood Church, one of the nation's largest, with a 16,000-seat arena.

As floodwaters rose, critics on social media asked why the doors of Lakewood Church stayed closed. Some even posted images and videos of the church from the outside that appeared to show parts of the area accessible, fueling a firestorm of questions about priorities and planning.

Osteen and church officials responded that Lakewood's building had flooding issues and that the church intended to open as a shelter once

---

45. The Gospel Coalition, "Prosperity Gospel Born in the USA," November 14, 2018, https://www.thegospelcoalition.org/article/prosperity-gospel-born-in-the-usa/.
46. Edge Induced Cohesion, "White Paper: The Negative Effects of the Prosperity Gospel on Those Who Fail to Prosper," August 24, 2025.

city and county shelters were full. Still, according to NPR and other observers, the building was reported closed to evacuees as late as the following Tuesday morning, despite the church's social media statements (catastrophic flooding in Houston began Saturday night). Only after mounting criticism and national headlines did Lakewood open its doors.

To be fair, as reported by multiple outlets, Lakewood and Osteen's team did eventually provide valuable help, organizing volunteers, gathering donations, and supporting recovery. But the delayed response left many questioning why a church of that size and prominence—empowered by the prosperity gospel—wasn't first in, rather than last.[47]

Critics, not the author, argue that the events illustrated a theological disconnect: if faith and riches are meant as evidence of God's blessing, why did the nation's wealthiest ministries lag behind those simply motivated by a sense of duty to their neighbors?

This debate isn't just about one church and one pastor. It exposes the deepest tension of prosperity teaching: promising divine favor to the comfortable and blaming hardship on the vulnerable, while sometimes failing to show up when the real-world need is greatest. For many observers, it was a clarifying moment, a reminder that Scripture calls for humility, quick mercy, and tangible action, not just wealth or televised prayer.

DUELING BIBLES: THE CONSERVATIVE CHRISTIAN PERSPECTIVE

Within American Christianity, not all leaders agree on what the Bible says about wealth, responsibility, and the role of government. Leaders

---

47. NBC News, "Joel Osteen Defends Not Opening Lakewood Church in Houston to Flood Victims," August 28, 2017, https://www.nbcnews.com/storyline/hurricane-harvey/joel-osteen-defends-not-opening-megachurch-harvey-victims-n797036.

like Paula White, Joel Osteen, and financial counselor Dave Ramsey have spoken publicly against government support programs for the poor, emphasizing individual responsibility, diligent work, and faith-based giving.

Ralph Reed of the Faith and Freedom Coalition goes even further, advocating for what he calls a "Christian dominion" over society—including economics—rooted in patriarchal and capitalist values.[48]

Supporters of these perspectives often cite verses like:

- 2 Corinthians 8:9: "For you know the grace of our Lord Jesus Christ, that though he was rich, yet for your sakes he became poor, so that you by his poverty might become rich." They interpret this as a promise of material blessing for believers, though many biblical scholars contend Paul meant generosity and sacrificial giving, not a blanket guarantee of riches.

- John 10:10: "I came that they may have life, and may have it abundantly." For prosperity preachers, this signals that God wants followers to enjoy abundant, even financial, blessing. Others argue Jesus is pointing to spiritual, not material, abundance.

- Luke 6:38: "Give, and it will be given to you." This is commonly used to encourage donations—often to ministries—with the promise that giving will unlock financial blessings. Traditional interpretations, however, resist making God's favor transactional.

---

48. An Epidemic among My People: Religion, Politics, and COVID–19 in the United States, edited by Paul A. Djupe and Amanda Friesen, OAPEN, April 11, 2025, https://library.oapen.org/bitstream/handle/20.500.12657/61716/1/external_content.pdf.

- Mark 10:30: "He will receive one hundred times more now in this time: houses, brothers, sisters, mothers, children, and land, with persecutions; and in the age to come eternal life." Here, prosperity teachers see an investment scheme; mainstream theology sees the cost (and communal blessing) of true discipleship.

Critics, including theologians on both the right and left, claim that prosperity-oriented teaching often takes such verses out of context. The broader biblical witness, they argue, calls for generosity, careful stewardship, and warns powerfully against greed, offering spiritual hope but not a formula for wealth.

The practical effect? When Christians hold such different views about what the Bible teaches—some stressing personal prosperity, others self-help, and others collective care—these beliefs shape how people vote, what kinds of laws get passed, which government programs the public supports or opposes, and, ultimately, how our society responds to those in need. In other words, religious disagreements don't just stay inside churches because they have real consequences for national policy and for the lives of poor and vulnerable Americans.

PROGRESSIVE AND MAINLINE CHRISTIAN PERSPECTIVE

Of course, many Christians see the economic and justice questions differently. Leaders such as economist Robert Reich, Rev. William Barber with the Poor People's Campaign, and Jim Wallis of Sojourners draw on both biblical tradition and economic analysis to argue that inequality is not inevitable, it is a product of deliberate policy choices that benefit the wealthy and powerful.

Robert Reich, former Secretary of Labor, regularly points out that a fairer system lifts everyone, not just those at the top. Rev. Barber's movement grounds itself in Jesus's mandate to care for the poor, pushing for living wages, expanded healthcare, and robust public education, not just charity, but structural change to break inherited cycles of poverty. Wallis and the Sojourners community insist that faith calls for accountability, not just generosity, where systems and leaders must answer for injustice, not just individuals for their choices.[49]

They draw heavily from Scripture's calls to "[judge] the cause of the poor and needy" (Jeremiah 22:16), "love … your neighbor as yourself" (Luke 10:27), and Jesus's own words in Matthew 25:40: "Because you did fit to one of the least of these my brothers, you did it to me." For these Christians, following Jesus means advocating for the marginalized, repairing broken systems, and ensuring that our laws and budgets reflect compassion and fairness.

This moral divide is not just theological; it plays out in policy debates, budget fights, and street-level politics. Every American, and every Christian, faces the same core question: Will faith be used to justify the status quo and protect the few, or to demand a society where justice and compassion shape every corner of life?

WHY WE CREATE "OTHERS," AND HOW IT SHAPES JUSTICE

Humans have always sorted the world into *us* versus *them*, a survival instinct that's terrible for justice. Leaders have long used fear of "the other" to gain power, scapegoating immigrants, minorities, or anyone

---

49. Robert Lassalle-Klein, "The Legacy of White Racism" in America's Original Sin, Sojourners, 1992, https://files.eric.ed.gov/fulltext/ED358227.pdf.

who doesn't fit their narrative. Today, the same reflex drives battles over policing, voting, and schools, hitting communities of color hardest.[50]

But "othering" cracks when real connection happens. Remember that Massachusetts graduation where neighbors—not just activists—showed up for Marcelo Gomes da Silva, a teen detained by ICE? Suddenly, the debate wasn't abstract; it was personal and close to home. Jesus saw it too: he broke down walls, uplifted outsiders, and shattered the idea that God's love stops at the tribe's edge.[51]

Bottom line: When faith is used to draw lines instead of build bridges, justice falters and the Gospel takes a hit.

THE ROOTS (AND RISKS) OF POLARIZATION

Why does every debate now feel like an endless knife fight? Some tribalism is ancient, but modern faith and politics have supercharged it. In the Reagan era, alliances between the Religious Right and Republican Party—amplified by groups like the Moral Majority—turned church issues like abortion and LGBTQ+ rights into partisan battle cries, and faith itself into a political weapon.

At the same time, many progressives recoiled, seeing faith as exclusive or dangerous. So, both sides built higher walls, defining themselves against an "enemy" and not building any bridges. When faith marries party, dialogue collapses. Differences turn to suspicions. Neighbors become rivals. We lose the community that makes democracy work, and we let cynical politicians profit from division.

---

50. Gary Fields, Associated Press, "From legislative chambers to schools, democracy for Black Americans is under attack, report finds," PBS NewsHour, April 15, 2023, https://www.pbs.org/newshour/politics/from-legislative-chambers-to-schools-democracy-for-black-americans-is-under-attack-report-finds.

51. CNN, "A community rallies for the release of a beloved high schooler detained by ICE," June 3, 2025, https://www.cnn.com/2025/06/03/us/massachusetts-gomes-da-silva-detained.

If that's the endgame, everyone loses. Again, let's return to the Jesus Principle as a filter. When evaluating any debate, run it through these four questions:

1. Does the fruit of the Spirit naturally arise?

Big promises aren't enough; look at what policies actually produce. If "reforms" make schools worse, neighborhoods meaner, or leave workers scrambling, is that real kindness, joy, or peace? Some argue these policies promote initiative; others see only anxiety and stress. The real test: Does love show up not just in church, but in classrooms and kitchens? If it doesn't, maybe fruit isn't what's growing.

2. Am I caring for the vulnerable?

Jesus's ministry started at the margins. When schools go underfunded, social supports vanish, and the voiceless wind up ignored, it's always the most vulnerable who lose. Both sides say they care for "the least of these." But the real test isn't declarations, it's who's left carrying the weight. If the floor drops out for struggling kids and families, the filter's failed.

3. Would I want this done to me—or to those I love?

The Golden Rule matters most when it pinches. Could you accept a world where your family had to choose between rent and food while others argue "sacrifice builds character?" Christ calls for empathy, not scapegoating. If you'd fight a system for your loved ones, why tolerate it for your neighbor? When empathy gets real, so does justice.

4. Is it true?

Truth is the backbone of the Gospel. Jesus exposed injustice and didn't flinch at uncomfortable facts, even when it cut against tradition.

Are we willing to face ugly realities—about inequality, exclusion, and whose interests get protected—or do we hide behind slogans? Following Jesus sometimes means naming hard truths and refusing easy comfort, especially when a system's winners and losers are plain to see.

THE JESUS PRINCIPLE AS A FILTER: WHAT TO TOSS, WHAT TO KEEP

A compass sets our direction, but the filter separates Gospel truth from cultural baggage. The filter asks: Does this policy or belief build justice, dignity, and opportunity, or does it reinforce walls and widen divides?

Toss out:

- School funding schemes that starve poor districts and leave classrooms crowded
- Voucher systems that drain resources from public schools and leave disadvantaged kids behind
- Policies or rhetoric that blame communities of color for structural inequality
- Practices that treat poverty as a personal failure instead of a challenge for the whole community
- Attitudes that protect comfort, privilege, or the status quo at the expense of others' future

Keep:

- Funding reforms that prioritize the most neglected schools and students
- Honest conversations about race, history, and privilege, even when uncomfortable

- Community-based support: mentorship, volunteering, school partnerships, and material aid for families
- Restorative justice and programs that bridge gaps, welcome outsiders, and expand opportunities
- Leadership that risks political capital to confront exclusion and repair what's been broken

Whenever a law or argument claims "Christian values," run it through this filter. If the policy deepens divisions, lets inequality persist, or keeps the gates shut—toss it. If it widens access, risks comfort to fix injustice, and stretches compassion across every boundary—keep it. That's the soil justice and the Gospel both need to grow in.

BOTTOM LINE

The true gospel in education, race, and equity isn't about protecting what we've got. It's about flinging open doors and making sure not one child gets left out because of where they live or the color of their skin.

CONCLUSION: RECLAIMING JUSTICE AND OPPORTUNITY

"It is easier to build strong children than to repair broken men."[52] Frederick Douglass's words ring truer than ever and serve as a warning. Justice is not a policy; it's the story we write for the next generation. Imagine an America where Jamal, and every kid, wakes up with the

---

52. This popular quote is widely attributed to Frederick Douglass, the nineteenth-century abolitionist and social reformer. While it expresses the spirit of Douglass's beliefs and writings about education and human development, some scholars note that it is not found verbatim in his published works, but rather paraphrases Douglass's themes about prevention and upbringing.

same hope and the same open door. That future is within reach, but only if we are bold enough to build it.

Redemption starts when we filter out policies and beliefs that harm the vulnerable and double down on those reflecting Christ's compassion and justice. Does that mean prioritizing public schools, tackling poverty at its roots, and building an economy where families can truly get ahead? This isn't just politics; it's backpacks, paychecks, and whether families make rent.

The choice ahead is stark: perpetuate cycles of exclusion and lost promise or rise to reclaim the common good. If we stall, the verdict will be written by what we leave behind: locked doors, squandered dreams, and a legacy of injustice. But if we act, side by side, we can write a new story: one where justice belongs to everyone, and opportunity really does reach all.

Imagine Jamal—not just surviving, but graduating with honors, launching a business, standing on a stage that was once locked to him, and showing every kid coming after that those heavy doors can swing wide.

Expansive goodwill isn't just a slogan. It's rolling up sleeves for Jamal, meeting him in the hallways of crumbling schools, and refusing to walk past families facing locked doors and broken dreams. It's communities, churches, and leaders partnering for real change, working side by side to tutor, mentor, advocate, and open doors that seemed forever closed. That's what modeling gospel action looks like in practice.

Now is not the time for safe gestures or shallow talk. The Jesus Principle demands more if America wants to move closer to its best promise: challenge indifference, strip away self-interest, and build systems that make room—real room—for every Jamal, every mother working three jobs, every single overlooked soul.

Let's build a country where no one is told: the door is locked for you. Because in the end, the Jesus Principle filter isn't just a message for policy; it's a call to open every door wider, until justice and dignity belong to all.

CHAPTER 5

WHO IS MY NEIGHBOR?

NO WARNING, NO MERCY

The pounding on the door hit at 4:17 a.m. Daniela, barely fifteen, snapped awake as ICE agents burst into the family's apartment. "¡Manos arriba!" they barked, rifles raised, the flashlight glare cutting the dark.

Her heart slammed against her ribs as boots thundered down the hallway.

Next thing she knew, her older brother Miguel—a DACA recipient, her big-hearted hero, and almost a nurse—was dragged to the curb in nothing but his boxers.

Miguel looked back once—eyes wide, searching for his family—before agents pressed his face to the pavement; his textbooks spilled out on the dew-soaked lawn. By sunrise, he was gone.

No warning. No charges. Just vanished, leaving Daniela's family gutted and the whole apartment block in shock.

Daniela's college admissions essay—"*I Want to Heal People Like My Brother*"—now gathers dust under her bed. For her, even the classroom feels menacing, and church—once a sanctuary—is just another space crawling with risk.

Her mother, a housekeeper, skips work shifts, heart pounding every time she glimpses an ICE checkpoint. "We're not criminals," Daniela whispers into her pillow most nights.

"We just want to live. To work. To survive."

This story is becoming a cruel, familiar pattern, and one that gnaws at the conscience of any nation, and, honestly, anyone who claims to follow Jesus.

In northern California, a friend named Francisco clocks three jobs just to keep food on the table. Quiet guy, kind face. He would give you the shirt off his back. He's undocumented, which, for a lot of folks, is all it takes to slap the "criminal" label on him, before they hear his story or shake his hand.

But like Miguel's family, Francisco lives on a hair-trigger; every knock at the door, every unexpected summons at work, chills him to the bone. ICE shows up, and you might never see your family again.

For millions, immigration isn't just a cable-news debate, it's what keeps them up at night, every single night. But Daniela's family isn't unique. This is happening in cities, towns, and borderlands across the nation.

A CROSSROADS OF CONSCIENCE

America's immigration system isn't just broken; it's cracked wide open and patched over by good intentions and campaign trail promises from both parties. For decades, Democrats and Republicans alike have passed the buck, failing to craft real reform that accounts for both the nation's undeniable labor needs and the basic humanity of those drawn here seeking a better life. Meanwhile, millions remain in perpetual limbo—working, building, hoping, fearing—with no actual path to belonging.

Let's name the gap: For generations, the country has thrived on immigrant labor, loving the fruits while ignoring the roots. We order dinner, check out at the pharmacy, drop kids at day care, all thanks to neighbors who aren't given a seat at the table.

As a nation, when we benefit from millions of residents while denying them basic security, we incur a moral debt we can no longer dodge. So, here's the crossroads: Will America finally take responsibility for the complicated reality it helped create, or keep shrugging, leaving millions to dangle on a thread they can neither cut nor climb?

Robert P. Jones, in *White Too Long*, puts his finger on something Americans usually whisper: the fear that's driving immigration gridlock is less about "values" and more about losing a long-standing racial pecking order.[53] It isn't just unease with change, but the fear of losing a version of America defined by whiteness and its privileges.

And you see this play out in the real world: policies like the 2025 travel ban, which targeted countries with mostly Black and brown populations, and the recent sweep of racial profiling under the current Trump administration, where people get stopped, questioned,

---

53. Robert P. Jones, *White Too Long: The Legacy of White Supremacy in American Christianity* (New York: Simon & Schuster, 2020).

and detained because of their language, accent, or the color of their skin—proof and due process be damned.[54]

Now, let's be clear: countries have a right to secure their borders. I grew up in Canada, where national borders are taken seriously, and they should be. Do you leave your front door unlocked so anyone can enter at night while you and your family are asleep? I don't think so.

The real question—the one staring back at us as followers of Jesus—is how we do it. Do we honor Christ's example by showing up in the middle of the night with masks and rifles, dragging out college kids and grandmothers, a reality you didn't hear about if you live in a Fox News conservative media bubble? Does state-sanctioned panic—children torn from parents, neighborhoods living in siege—line up with the Gospel's call to love, mercy, and justice? Or could we chart a better way, one that honors the rule of law without losing our soul?

To even begin answering, we have to face the real complexity, not the caricatures, the tangled, contradictory Christian convictions that shape America's immigration crisis.

DUELING BIBLES: CONSERVATIVE CHRISTIAN PERSPECTIVE

Let's talk about the pews, the pulpits, and the policy tables. Among many conservative Christians, the debate around immigration isn't just about headlines, it's a matter of biblical principle, patriotism, and the persistent anxiety that if the nation loses control, chaos follows fast. Leaders like Reverend Samuel Rodriguez of the National

---

54. Trump administration, "Proclamation—A New Travel Ban Targeting Black and Brown Majority Countries," June 2025, National Immigration Law Center, https://www.nilc.org/articles/trumps-newest-xenophobic-travel-ban/; see also Amnesty International, "Trump's Travel Ban Will Harm People Seeking Safety," June 2025, https://www.amnesty.org/en/latest/news/2025/06/usa-trumps-travel-ban-will-harm-people-seeking-safety/.

Hispanic Christian Leadership Conference, Robert Jeffress at First Baptist Dallas (and longtime Trump advisor), Tony Perkins from the Family Research Council, and powerhouses like the Heritage Foundation don't just quote Scripture: they build their worldview around it.

For them, the rule of law isn't just a civic virtue; it's divine order. "Let every soul be in subjection to the higher authorities, for there is no authority except from God" (Romans 13:1–3). The logic lands hard: looking the other way on more than 10 million undocumented neighbors, they argue, frays the rope that ties society together. If mercy washes out law, what remains? Their fear: that lax borders will unravel justice, national security, maybe even the shared values that define America.

Some of these convictions draw on real-world stories, sometimes tragic ones. Recent headlines about a felony murder conviction against an undocumented worker in Georgia who killed a mother of five land with the weight of grim proof: "See? This is why we need ICE. This is why order comes first."[55]

And then there's the stew of policy and myth: beliefs that undocumented immigrants overload welfare rolls, drive hospitals into the ground, and sap state budgets of billions, which are all themes Heritage Foundation scholars report (with much debate) when they estimate net fiscal costs above $150 billion a year.[56] Never mind, say critics, that many of these estimates count the U.S.-born children

---

55. Man accused of killing Georgia mother was in the US illegally, authorities say," CNN, March 23, 2025, https://www.cnn.com/2025/03/23/us/georgia-mother-killing-us-illegally; see also "Illegal immigrant charged with killing Georgia grandmother in random attack," Fox News, March 21, 2025, https://www.foxnews.com/us/illegal-immigrant-released-biden-admin-charged-killing-georgia-grandmother-random-attack.

56. Heritage Foundation, "The Fiscal Cost of Unlawful Immigrants and Amnesty to the U.S. Taxpayer," https://www.heritage.org/immigration/report/the-fiscal-cost-unlawful-immigrants-and-amnesty-the-us-taxpayer; see also Cato Institute, "The Fiscal Impact of Immigration in the United States," https://www.cato.org/white-paper/fiscal-impact-immigration-united-states.

of immigrants, or that multiple nonpartisan analysts calculate a net gain when all taxes and labor are weighed on the same scale. Still, the narrative persists, feeding both policy and the polls.

Here's where Scripture gets loaded up like ammunition:

- "Those who forsake the law praise the wicked" (Proverbs 28:4)
- "Subject yourselves to every ordinance of man for the Lord's sake" (1 Peter 2:13–14)
- "Remind them to be in subjection to rulers and to authorities" (Titus 3:1)
- "Give therefore to Caesar the things that are Caesar's" (Matthew 22:21)
- "If anyone is unwilling to work, don't let him eat" (2 Thessalonians 3:10)
- "It is joy to the righteous to do justice, but it is a destruction to the workers of iniquity" (Proverbs 21:15)

Policy follows: more ICE raids, taller walls, an end to DACA and birthright citizenship, firm opposition to anything that smells like "amnesty." It's not about cruelty—at least not in intent—so much as about drawing thick lines and keeping the house in order.

"Loving our neighbor means demanding they enter legally; anything less enables coyotes and cartels." That's what a deacon told me in Texas as he bowed in prayer for the safety of migrants, with even his own family pitching in to drive folks back to the border. Compassion, yes—but only after accountability.

Let's not slide into stereotypes. These are not, in most cases, heartless people. They're worried about social trust, the rule of law, and the risk that open doors enable tragedies, from human trafficking, child exploitation, to cartel violence. They want security first, not simply out of fear, but out of moral duty as they see it.

But here's where it gets tricky: while progressives weigh the Golden Rule ("Would I want deportation for my family?"), conservatives flip the script ("Would I want my tax dollars and laws subverted, the queue ignored?"). Both sides grab hold of the same Jesus and point Him in opposite directions.

PROGRESSIVE AND MAINLINE CHRISTIAN PERSPECTIVE: MERCY WITHOUT BORDERS

But that's only half the church pews. On the other end, a chorus of progressive and mainline Christians sees hardline immigration enforcement as a profound betrayal of the Gospel. These are voices like Rev. Liz Theoharis of the Poor People's Campaign, Rev. Jim Wallis from Sojourners, and Rev. Jacqui Lewis of Middle Collegiate Church in New York City. They're joined by organizations like the Evangelical Immigration Table—a coalition of ten evangelical denominations—and Church World Service, representing millions of everyday Christians across the country.

Here, the call is for hospitality, not hostility. These leaders say the Bible is clear: God's people have always been "strangers in a strange land." Jesus? A refugee, chased out of town with his family (Matthew 2:13–15). And his whole ministry? Busting open the barriers between "insiders" and "outsiders."

So what's the scriptural foundation?

- The parable of the Good Samaritan (Luke 10:25–37): the

hero is the one who stops, helps, and shows mercy, not the one who clings to religious or national purity

- "If a stranger lives as a foreigner with you ... love him as yourself, for you lived as foreigners in the land of Egypt" (Leviticus 19:33–34)

- "I was a stranger, and you welcomed me" (Matthew 25:35)

- "He executes justice for the fatherless and widow and loves the foreigner in giving him food and clothing. Therefore, love the foreigner, for you were foreigners in the land of Egypt" (Deuteronomy 10:18–19)

- "Don't oppress ... the foreigner" (Zechariah 7:10)

- "Don't forget to show hospitality to strangers, for in doing so, some have entertained angels without knowing it" (Hebrews 13:2)

- "There is neither Jew or Greek ... slave nor free man ... male nor female" (Galatians 3:28)

For these communities, welcoming asylum seekers is not policy, it's the heartbeat of faith. "When Jesus says, 'I was a stranger and you invited me in,'" says Wallis, "he's not drafting a plank for the Democratic Party. He's laying down the core of Christian discipleship."[57]

Stats matter here, too: undocumented immigrants paid nearly $97 billion in U.S. taxes in 2022 and $90 billion in 2023. And the narrative that immigrants are dangerous? Multiple studies show they're

---

57. Jim Wallis, *Christ in Crisis: Why We Need to Reclaim Jesus* (San Francisco: HarperOne, 2019), 150.

less likely to commit crimes than native-born citizens, plus most can't access programs like SNAP or Medicaid.[58]

While the "cost" debate rages, progressive and evangelical supporters point at billions paid in taxes and their essential roles in every sector, from hospitals to tech. The real crisis, they insist, is not at the border, but in Washington's failure to create a rational, humane system.

This isn't soft-hearted naiveté. These Christians want justice with teeth. They push for a real pathway to citizenship, end for-profit detention centers, and invest in addressing root causes abroad: poverty, violence, and climate change. And even here, ninety percent of evangelical Christians back both secure borders and humane, legal pathways.[59]

I still remember talking to a nanny pool and young mom group at a playground in the San Francisco Bay Area where I live. One, clutching her toddler, told me quietly, "I pray every day that America will see us as neighbors, not as threats." That prayer, that ache, echoes through sanctuaries and kitchen tables all over the country.

Of course, deep divisions remain within the church, as in the nation. Some see hospitality and justice as central; others fear cultural change and disorder. The challenge—maybe the only hope—is

---

58. Institute on Taxation and Economic Policy, "Undocumented Immigrants Paid $96.7 Billion in U.S. Taxes in 2022," https://itep.org/undocumented-immigrants-taxes-2024/; American Immigration Council, "Undocumented immigrants paid nearly $90 billion in taxes in 2023," https://www.americanimmigrationcouncil.org/press-release/immigrants-keep-economy-strong-as-congress-debates-mass-deportation/; PMC, "Comparing crime rates between undocumented immigrants, legal immigrants, and native-born citizens," https://pmc.ncbi.nlm.nih.gov/articles/PMC7768760/; American Immigration Council, "Debunking the Myth of Immigrants and Crime," https://www.americanimmigrationcouncil.org/fact-sheet/debunking-myth-immigrants-and-crime/.

59. Lifeway Research, "2025 Evangelical Views on Immigration Study," https://research.lifeway.com/wp-content/uploads/2025/02/2025-Evangelical-Views-on-Immigration-Report.pdf; see also Baptist News Global, "Evangelicals more open to immigration than their politicians believe," https://baptistnews.com/article/evangelicals-more-open-to-immigration-than-their-politicians-believe/.

for Christians of all types to bridge those divides, seeking a justice that honors both the Bible and democracy.

And that's where the Jesus Principle comes in, a unifying lens for beliefs and policies that, for once, could actually move the needle.

THE JESUS PRINCIPLE AS A COMPASS

If the shouting matches and dueling verses haven't swayed this country, maybe it's because we're asking the wrong question. If we're tired of fighting over verses, maybe it's time to put down the weapons and listen for direction: What gets us closer to Jesus, not just in theory but in action? That's the real compass. And if the way forward isn't clear, maybe the next question to ask is what needs to be filtered out along the way.

THE JESUS PRINCIPLE AS A FILTER

Here's how the Jesus Principle gets practical: think of the four core aspects, straight from the Gospels and the writings of St. Paul, and lived in Jesus's actions. These aren't the only questions you can ask, but they are the ones that break the cycle of proof-text wars and force us to face the heart of the matter as we work to filter out toxins that can hurt us, while keeping what is nourishing and life giving.

1. *Does shutting out and scapegoating immigrants build justice, safety, and peace, or just more fear and division?*

When ICE separates families in the dead of night or leaves parents and children never to be reunited, can we honestly point to any fruit of the Spirit? If our laws breed terror and trauma, are we sure that's not the fruit of fear instead?

2. Are we protecting the people who pick our food, build our homes, and care for our loved ones, or making life hell for anyone who is "different"?

Jesus's entire ministry was about moving toward those shoved to the margins, seen most clearly in passages like Matthew 9, where "he was moved with compassion for them because they were harassed and scattered, like sheep without a shepherd." Care, in Jesus-speak, isn't handouts. It's repair, welcome, and dignity.

3. Would you want your family, your neighbor—or any nonviolent, law-abiding person—dragged out of bed at night, detained, and separated from their kids, just for being undocumented or "looking suspicious"?

The Golden Rule isn't optional: "Do to others as you would have them do to you" (Luke 6:31). Imagine your family torn apart in the night, your child alone, your parent gone. If we wouldn't wish it on our own, how do we justify it for neighbors God made in the same image?

4. Is this really aligned with the life, teaching, and radical welcome of Jesus—or are we just protecting our privileges and telling ourselves it's necessary?

Jesus was all about hard truth, even if it meant calling out the powerful or unsettling the pious. In the real world, facts are on the table: immigrants, documented or not, are less likely to commit crimes, pay billions in taxes, and anchor communities from farm towns to city blocks. Distorted stories might feed fear, but they can't be confused for gospel truth. "The truth will set you free."

For Jesus, "neighbor" always means crossing a line, past comfort, past the law, into the risky space where solidarity and accountability meet. And that's the filter: anything less is, at best, a detour.

THE JESUS PRINCIPLE AS A FILTER: WHAT TO TOSS, WHAT TO KEEP

A compass shows us direction. But a filter clears the toxins from the cup. Following Jesus means more than aiming at a goal; it means sifting out what poisons both our politics and our faith.

Toss out:

- Language that labels people "illegals" or treats newcomers as outsiders
- Scapegoating immigrants to dodge deeper economic or policy problems
- Punitive policies or raids that humiliate or dehumanize
- Indifference to violence, poverty, or foreign policy at migration's root

Keep:

- Fair but firm borders with humane enforcement
- Security screening for those who pose real threats, but also recognizing most newcomers seek safety and opportunity
- Hospitality and practical help when possible, like the Good Samaritan, regardless of paperwork
- Justice that combines order and practical pathways (citizenship, legal protection, community support)
- Consistent respect for the dignity and humanity of every person, documented or not

BOTTOM LINE

Strength and compassion aren't opposites. True security enforces law without losing our soul: guarding borders, yes, but never treating people as less than neighbors.

A BETTER WAY: POLICIES ROOTED IN DIGNITY

For generations, America turned a blind eye while immigrant families helped build our economy, harvesting food, staffing hospitals, raising children, and rebuilding after disasters. Millions filled jobs few others took, hired year after year by companies that depended on their labor but looked the other way when paperwork didn't add up. Our communities grew and prospered from their work, yet our laws never matched reality.

When the debate turns to "illegal" status and shutting the door, it's as if our nation forgets its decades-long role in encouraging people to put down roots. The truth is, we are complicit: corporations, farms, private homes recruited season after season, while policies lagged far behind. Pretending we can simply flip a switch now—evict families, shutter businesses, tear apart communities—is denial, not justice. It's like a landlord cashing rent for years, then tossing out tenants over paperwork. Both the tenant and landlord are caught in the results, but only one holds the real power to change it.

If the Jesus Principle is our compass, real dignity and accountability must lead the way. Secure borders are possible, but not at the cost of mercy. Practical, bipartisan reforms like the Dignity Act and Evangelical Immigration Table recommend restitution, earned legalization, background checks, and prioritizing citizenship for Dreamers. Enforcement should target true public safety threats, not Sunday school teachers, farm hands, or the pregnant mom who's been working in the same town for a decade. Canada and other nations prove it can be done by rewarding skills, supporting families, and balancing national needs with compassion.

We can't solve immigration by only focusing on border management; we have to invest in hope, addressing why families leave Honduras, Guatemala, or El Salvador in the first place by confronting violence, poverty, and lost economic opportunity with real aid and partnership.

There is another way: one in which churches, mayors, and Congress choose humility and courage. Imagine a system that owns our history and gives every child, every Dreamer, every parent a fair shot at belonging. The blueprints are there, the evidence is clear, and the only thing missing is the will to choose policies rooted in dignity, not in delay.

CONCLUSION: CHOOSING OUR LEGACY

So here's where it all lands. The questions staring us down—at church, in Congress, and at the kitchen table—cut deeper than any soundbite. Will we be remembered for walls, raids, and fear, or for building bridges of justice and compassion that last? The prophet's call still echoes: "Let justice roll down like waters, and righteousness like an ever-flowing stream" (Amos 5:24), but it's up to us to decide what kind of justice will define our time.

Miguel's family still prays for his return. Sofia still dreams of college. Neighborhoods in every ZIP code wait to see if America will keep treating immigrants like skeletons in the closet, or as neighbors worth knowing, people worth standing up for. Will this country take responsibility for the system it built, or keep leaving millions in limbo, hoping someone else finds the courage to fix the mess?

This is a legacy moment. The future will measure us not just by what laws we pass, but also by the courage and grace with which we enforce them. The real test: Did we choose fear or dignity, cruelty or the way of Christ?

As the dust settles, may we summon the grit to love our neighbors, the honesty to face our history, and the boldness to build something better, for ourselves, our children, and every stranger we dare to call neighbor.

CHAPTER 6

STEWARDSHIP OR EXPLOITATION?

FAITH IN A BURNING WORLD

The sky outside Anna's window looked like the end of the world: rust-red sun blotted by smoke, ash drifting down and clinging to every breath. Somewhere, her little brother's cough broke the hush of a land waiting for rain. Their family's fields, green for generations, were now brittle and brown. Even the creek was just cracked mud.

It wasn't the apocalypse—no one said as much—but Anna felt the word hovering at the edge of her thoughts. At church, elders prayed for rain but warned about "climate alarmism." Her pastor insisted God was in control; her science teacher said the world was changing, and people were a big part of it.

Anna wondered if faith meant staying silent or seeing more clearly than ever.

One evening, she turned her grandmother's Bible to Psalm 24: "The earth is the Lord's, and everything in it." Meant for comfort, those words now pressed more questions.

Anna prayed—not just for rain, but for courage, for wisdom to see what faith required now, and for a church that counted caring for creation as blessing, not heresy.

Anna isn't alone. Versions of her story echo everywhere: in avoided conversations and the hush after another failed harvest. Yet hope appears too. Anna found others in her church with the same questions. Together, they planted trees, pitched in together, and learned that real change often starts quietly, even when the world outside feels overwhelming.

THE CRISIS IN NUMBERS

The world Anna prays for is the world all of us wake up to now. The climate crisis is no longer a specter, but our daily reality. Since the first smokestacks of the Industrial Revolution, global temperatures have increased by as much as 2.3°F (1.3°C). In 2024, we crossed a new threshold: our first year with global temperatures averaging above 2.7°F (1.5°C) over old baselines.[60]

---

60. NASA, "Global Temperature | Vital Signs—Climate Change," https://climate.nasa.gov/vital-signs/global-temperature/; World Meteorological Organization, "WMO confirms 2024 as warmest year on record at about 1.55°C above pre-industrial level," https://wmo.int/news/media-centre/wmo-confirms–2024-warmest-year-record-about–155degc-above-pre-industrial-level; Berkeley Earth, "Global Temperature Report for 2024," https://berkeleyearth.org/global-temperature-report-for–2024/.

NASA, "Global Temperature | Vital Signs—Climate Change," https://climate.nasa.gov/vital-signs/global-temperature/; World Meteorological Organization, "WMO confirms 2024 as warmest year on record at about 1.55°C above pre-industrial level," https://wmo.int/news/media-centre/wmo-confirms–2024-warmest-year-record-about–155degc-above-pre-industrial-level; Berkeley Earth, "Global Temperature Report for 2024," https://berkeleyearth.org/global-temperature-report-for–2024/.

These numbers are easy to skim past, but their weight hangs heavy. Under that extra half-degree, the future teeters: Will coral reefs hang on, protecting coastal fisheries, or collapse entirely? Will crops feed the hungry, or will drought and famine become the new normal in places once blessed with plenty?

The extremes don't just multiply, they concentrate. Hurricanes grow wetter and meaner, fueled by record-warm oceans. Sea levels, up eight inches since 1900, threaten to rise another one to four feet by the century's end, threatening to redraw coastlines from Louisiana to Bangladesh.

But as Anna has seen, the fallout never lands fairly. In Phoenix, families crowd emergency rooms to escape triple-digit heat. In Florida, single mothers fend off flooding with each hurricane. In Iowa, elderly farmers watch their topsoil turn to dust. Across the globe in Bangladesh, saltwater seeps into wells, leaving entire communities scrambling for drinkable water.

Yet, against this bleak arithmetic, examples of resilience appear, with community cooling centers opening in heat-stricken cities, churches offering shelter during storms, local farmers experimenting with drought-resistant seeds, and new hope coming from the energy transition. Today, wind and solar power are not just cleaner, but are also the cheapest forms of new electricity in most of the world, costing less than coal and, increasingly, even natural gas. Renewable energy sources—like solar, wind, and now even offshore wind—make it easier than ever to choose a sustainable path.[61] Amid the numbers and headlines, lives and choices unfold, proof that hope and action are never entirely out of reach.

---

61. International Renewable Energy Agency, "Around 90% of renewables cheaper than fossil fuels worldwide," https://www.reuters.com/business/energy/around–90-renewables-cheaper-than-fossil-fuels-worldwide-irena-says–2025-07–22/; Lazard, "Lazard Releases 2025 Levelized Cost of Energy+ Report," https://www.lazard.com/news-announcements/lazard-releases–2025-levelized-cost-of-energyplus-report-pr/; UN/IRENA, "Renewables the Cheapest Electricity Source in 2024," https://energytracker.asia/un-and-irena-renewables-the-cheapest-electricity-source/.

THE SCIENCE OF CRISIS: TIPPING POINTS AND CLIMATE LAG

So where does all this chaos begin? Strip away the headlines, and the story boils down to a truth any grade schooler would recognize: When we burn coal, oil, and gas, carbon dioxide (CO_2) is released. That CO_2 wraps our planet in a warming blanket, trapping heat that would otherwise escape.

But Earth isn't just a victim—it resists. Oceans, forests, and frozen permafrost work as heat sinks, each absorbing the excess CO_2. Oceans alone have sponged up about ninety percent of the extra heat. Still, even the best sponge eventually saturates. As it fills, the rules of daily life are rewritten, and stored heat spills back out, intensifying weather and raising temperatures for decades to come.[62]

CLIMATE LAG: WHAT IS IT?

Climate lag means there's a built-in delay between when greenhouse gases are released and when their full impact is felt. Almost half of the CO_2 released by burning fossil fuels is absorbed by the oceans, which act as giant thermal sponges. But oceans are slow to warm up—and even slower to cool down—so they hang onto that heat and carbon for decades before gradually releasing it. Think of a pot of soup: you can turn off the stove and it will stay hot for a long time.[63]

---

62. NOAA, "Climate Change: Ocean Heat Content," https://www.climate.gov/news-features/understanding-climate/climate-change-ocean-heat-content; NASA, "Ocean Warming | Vital Signs—Climate Change," https://climate.nasa.gov/vital-signs/ocean-warming/; Max Planck Society, "Arctic Permafrost in Climate Change," https://www.mpg.de/23899031/permafrost-climate-change.

63. NOAA, "Climate Change: Ocean Heat Content," https://www.climate.gov/news-features/understanding-climate/climate-change-ocean-heat-content; NASA, "Ocean Warming | Vital Signs—Climate Change," https://climate.nasa.gov/vital-signs/ocean-warming/; NASA Science, "The Ocean and Climate Change," https://science.nasa.gov/earth/explore/the-ocean-and-climate-change/; Earth Observatory, "Thermal inertia in the climate system—Earth's Big Heat Bucket," https://earthobservatory.nasa.gov/features/HeatBucket/heatbucket4.php.

What does this mean for us? Even if emissions stopped today, warming would keep going for up to four more decades while the oceans slowly released their stored heat. The climate we're living in now is actually the result of pollution from decades ago, and what we emit now will shape the climate that our children and grandchildren inherit.

Climate lag makes progress feel slow and, at times, deeply discouraging because we're living both with our own choices and with the delayed consequences of the past. That's why urgent action is critical, even if the results aren't instant, and why every bit of reduction—cutting emissions, planting trees, switching to clean energy—matters for breaking the cycle.

POINTS OF NO RETURN

Already, the signs are indisputable. The Arctic is warming nearly four times faster than the rest of the planet, turning ancient ice to water and destabilizing global weather currents. This polar meltdown wobbles the jet stream, that invisible river of wind that usually guides the seasons. The result: weather chaos as the Midwest lurches from deep freezes to record heat, cities drown in rising tides, and wildfires chew relentlessly across the West.

Other dangers are brewing underground. Thawing Arctic permafrost is releasing methane, a greenhouse gas eighty times more potent than CO_2, like a slow-motion time bomb. It's not distant speculation: ice is vanishing, currents are shifting, and that permafrost bomb could be triggered within a generation if communities, governments, and churches ignore both science and lived witness.[64]

---

64. Yale Sustainability, "Methane is 80 times more potent than CO_2 in the first 20 years after release," https://sustainability.yale.edu/explainers/yale-experts-explain-methane-emissions; Smithsonian Magazine, "Permafrost Thaw in Siberia Creates a Ticking 'Methane Bomb,'" https://www.smithsonianmag.com/smart-news/ticking-timebomb-siberia-thawing-permafrost-releases-more-methane-180978381/; Arctic WWF, "Putting a lid on methane emissions before it's too late," https://www.arcticwwf.org/newsroom/features/putting-a-lid-on-methane-emissions-before-its-too-late/.

These are tipping points, ledges that, once crossed, cannot be reversed. Like falling dominoes, one precipitates another. The Stockholm Resilience Centre highlights over twenty, but six are the most urgent as we near 1.5°C global warming[65]:

- *Permafrost Thaw*: Ancient carbon and methane are released, rapidly accelerating warming worldwide.

- *Coral Reef Die-Off*: Heating and acidic seas bleach and kill corals, collapsing marine food supplies from Florida to the Great Barrier Reef.

- *Barents Sea Ice Loss*: Melting Arctic ice amplifies warming and throws North American and European weather patterns off balance.

- *Labrador Sea Current Collapse*: If the AMOC, the Atlantic's great conveyor belt, stutters, Europe's climate and global systems are thrown into turmoil.

- *Greenland Ice Sheet Collapse*: Full melting could raise seas by twenty-four feet over hundreds of years, submerging cities across continents.

- *West Antarctic Ice Sheet Collapse*: Major glaciers already destabilizing could add up to ten feet of sea level rise over hundreds of years.

---

65. Stockholm Resilience Centre, "World at risk of passing multiple climate tipping points above 1.5°C global warming," https://www.stockholmresilience.org/research/research-news/2022-09-08-world-at-risk-of-passing-multiple-climate-tipping-points-above–1.5c-global-warming.html; "Exceeding 1.5°C global warming could trigger multiple climate tipping points," https://www.stockholmresilience.org/publications/publications/2024-10-10-exceeding–1.5c-global-warming-could-trigger-multiple-climate-tipping-points.html; National Snow and Ice Data Center, "Why Ice Sheets Matter," https://nsidc.org/learn/parts-cryosphere/ice-sheets/why-ice-sheets-matter.

Beyond these, the Amazon—Earth's "lungs"—is close to its own turning point. A little more deforestation could flip it into dry savannah (grassland instead of rainforest), releasing even more stored carbon and disrupting rainfall worldwide.

Yet these grim cascades can still be interrupted. Evidence shows that both local and global action—restoring wetlands, reforming land use, advocating policy—builds resilience. Anna's congregation swapped its ancient furnace for solar panels after local students launched a "green week." It wasn't a cure-all, but it let science and faith walk side by side. Collective action still matters; it just has to happen now.

A MORAL DIVIDE AMONG CHRISTIANS

Genesis 1:28 divides Christians: "God blessed them, and God said to them, 'Be fruitful and multiply and fill the earth and subdue it and have dominion over the fish of the sea and over the birds of the air and over every living thing that moves upon the earth.'"

Some see "dominion" as a license to use resources and fuel industry; others read it as a mandate for stewardship and protection. The debate runs through every church: jobs versus healing, managing versus guarding. This single verse splits believers into opposing camps, each claiming to defend faith. When Scripture itself points both directions, the only way forward is to examine the arguments and their consequences.

DUELING BIBLES

The Conservative Christian Perspective

For many conservative Christians, climate change and environmental policy are understood and evaluated through a specific biblical lens, a worldview rooted in God's sovereignty, providence, and the unique place of human beings in creation. This perspective draws on several key passages from Scripture, which together create a framework skeptical of "climate doom," cautious about government intervention, and confident that earthly stability rests first and last with God, not humanity.

Consider the following foundational verses:

- Genesis 8:22: "While the earth remains, seedtime and harvest, and cold and heat, and summer and winter, and day and night will not cease." This verse is offered as reassurance that God has promised the ongoing order and reliability of nature's seasons for as long as the world lasts, implying that fears of catastrophic, irreversible change are ultimately misplaced.

- Genesis 9:11–13: "I will establish my covenant with you: all flesh will not be cut off any more by the waters of the flood; there will never again be a flood to destroy the earth. … I set my rainbow in the cloud, and it will be for a sign of a covenant between me and the earth." Here, conservative literalists find a divine guarantee that global floods—especially world-ending sea-level rise—are eternally off the table. They argue that God himself put boundaries on how much destruction the earth will face.

- Genesis 1:28: "God blessed them. God said to them, 'Be fruitful, multiply, fill the earth, and subdue it. Have dominion over the fish of the sea, over the birds of the sky, and over every living thing that moves on the earth.'" This "dominion mandate" is the classic biblical charter for human enterprise, resource development, and industrial progress. Any effort or policy that restricts these activities, especially out of fear of human-caused disaster, is weighed skeptically since God's blessing on stewardship is seen as inseparable from productivity.

- Job 38:8–11: "Or who shut up the sea with doors, when it broke out of the womb ... and said, 'You may come here, but no further. Your proud waves shall be stopped here?'" For many, this vivid image of God setting boundaries for the oceans serves as a theological brake on climate panic: if the Creator commands the tides, then talk of runaway, human-driven sea-level rise is regarded as an overstatement.

- Matthew 6:34: "Therefore don't be anxious for tomorrow, for tomorrow will be anxious for itself. Each day's own evil is sufficient." In response to alarm over possible future climate outcomes, many conservative pastors cite Jesus's admonition against worry. Christians are encouraged to reject fear-driven scenarios and instead trust in God's daily provision and sovereign plan.

- 2 Peter 3:10: "But the day of the Lord will come as a thief in the night, in which the heavens will pass away with a great noise, and the elements will be dissolved with fervent heat, and the earth and the works that are in it will be burned up." Finally, this is invoked as a definitive eschatological claim: yes, the world will end, but not because of humanity's carbon output; it will end at God's appointed time, by God's action, not human oversight or error.

This perspective does not threaten apathy; it still values stewardship and hard work. But it does produce skepticism of climate alarms, resistance to burdensome regulation, and above all, a focus on faith, responsibility, and the ultimate certainty that "God's hand is still on the thermostat." For conservative Christians, these passages from Scripture create a bedrock of confidence that frames all ecological debate.

The Progressive and Mainline Christian Perspective

Progressive and mainline Christians draw their vision of creation care from a rich tapestry of scriptural sources, emphasizing stewardship, interconnectedness, and the moral accountability of humans before God. Their argument is neither modern nor marginal. It flows straight from the text:

- Revelation 11:18: "... to destroy those who destroy the earth." God's judgment is pictured as falling not only on individual sinners but on systems—and societies—that devastate creation. For this tradition, ecological harm is a spiritual and moral violation, not simply a managerial failure. Justice, as seen in Revelation, requires actively resisting destruction and healing what has been broken.

- Proverbs 12:10: "A righteous man respects the life of his animal, but the tender mercies of the wicked are cruel." Compassionate care is not just for people but extends to all living creatures. Christians are called to honor life, minimize suffering, and reject patterns, whether in agriculture, commerce, or daily life that inflict needless harm on animals or the earth.

- Psalm 24:1: "The earth is Yahweh's, with its fullness; the world, and those who dwell in it." The logic of stewardship is rooted in God's ownership: the created world is not ours to possess or exploit, but a gift to be managed wisely and reverently for God's sake, and for future generations. Christians, therefore, must live as grateful, accountable caretakers.

- Genesis 2:15: "Yahweh God took the man, and put him into the garden of Eden to cultivate and keep it." This ancient commission is a touchstone for Christian ecology: we are tasked to serve, "cultivate," and "keep" (or protect) the earth with diligence and humility. Active care, not passive consumption, is the standard for Christian faithfulness.

- Hosea 4:1–3: "There is no truth … therefore the land will mourn … the animals of the field and the birds of the sky; yes, the fish of the sea also die." Prophetic tradition links environmental crisis directly to human injustice, dishonesty, and neglect. The land "mourns" because of our sins, an indictment still timely for the age of climate disruption and mass extinction.

- Romans 8:19–22: "The whole creation groans and travails in pain together until now." Creation's suffering is not just a metaphor, but a cosmic reality. All nature "groans" under the burden of human brokenness, longing for redemption. Christians—anticipating renewal—are called to begin that healing work now by relieving creation's pain wherever and however they can.

For progressive Christians, these verses define a mandate of repair and advocacy. Environmental harm is not a side issue; it is foundational to loving God and neighbor. The biblical story is not only about human souls but the flourishing of all creation, and faithfulness is measured by the care, justice, and restoration Christians bring to this "earth that is Yahweh's."

THE JESUS PRINCIPLE AS COMPASS

When it comes to how Christians respond to the climate crisis, the compass isn't found in slogans or party lines, it's in asking: Are our choices moving us toward the character and calling of Jesus, or away from it?

Jesus framed his life around far-reaching stewardship, neighbor-love, and a faith that acted for the good of all creation, not just our own tribe. If our faith simply defends comfort or cloaks neglect, we're off course. The compass of the Jesus Principle always asks: Does this decision extend care, humility, and hope, and not just for us, but for the most vulnerable and for the earth that belongs to God, as stated in Psalm 24? That's the north star for any gospel-shaped response to a burning world.

To use the Jesus Principle as a compass is to let Christ—not politics, tradition, or even personal comfort—set our direction. It's not about debating doctrine, but about following the One who healed, defended the vulnerable, and broke down barriers of indifference and fear. If the compass is working, every choice—personal or political—pulls us toward mercy, humility, and hope. That's how we move toward Jesus and not just circle the wagons while the world outside burns.

THE JESUS PRINCIPLE AS A FILTER

If the compass shows you what direction to aim, the filter shows you what's worth carrying and what's not. Plenty of beliefs, stories, and slogans sound right inside your own tribe, but try pouring them through the teachings of Jesus, and see what comes out the other side. Not everything will make it.

Imagine pouring water through a coffee filter. The filter's job is to catch the bitter grounds and let only the pure stuff through. The Jesus Principle works the same way. Before following a policy, a church tradition, or a clever argument, ask: Does this actually sound like the Jesus found in the Gospels? Does it leave bitterness, fear, or division behind, or does it produce compassion, humility, and real neighbor-love?

> **Author's Warning:** No one gets away with just quoting Jesus and feeling righteous. This is where things get interesting, and maybe a bit bloody. These questions cut against slogans and call out the real consequences. Let's see what happens when we hold up a gospel-shaped mirror.

1. Does this bear the fruit of the Spirit—or poison the well?

> **CONSERVATIVE CHRISTIAN:** Spiritual strength means offending people. If you worry more about comfort than conviction, you're lukewarm. Sometimes the Spirit calls for righteous anger and a spine of steel. Gentleness is fine, but not if it sells out truth. Unity matters, but not at the price of surrender.

> **PROGRESSIVE CHRISTIAN:** If church leaves people feeling shamed or blamed, that's rot, not righteousness. The Spirit heals, welcomes, and fights for hope. If what comes out is division or cruelty, call it poison. The Gospel is for the bruised, not another weapon. If your faith leaves more scars than healing, it's not of Jesus—it's toxic.

2. Does this protect the vulnerable—or hand them over?

> **CONSERVATIVE CHRISTIAN:** Real charity stays in the church,

not on government dole. Empower the poor, don't trap them in programs. Borders and strong families come first, or chaos wins. Blank checks breed dependency, not dignity. Love has limits; real help means tough boundaries.

PROGRESSIVE CHRISTIAN: If "order" makes the hungry hungrier or disaster victims homeless, that's not protection, it's self-preservation dressed up with Scripture. Climate change always hits the poor hardest. Jesus broke bread with the ones at the bottom and broke the rules for them. If love doesn't cost the powerful, it isn't love. Protecting the vulnerable means standing in the path of harm, not closing doors as the crisis rises.

3. Would I want this forced on my family?

CONSERVATIVE CHRISTIAN: Life isn't supposed to be easy. Without hard rules and discipline, you get chaos. Tough policies hurt, but they're what keep a nation strong. If the truth stings, it's probably exactly what's needed. The next generation needs backbone, not endless comfort.

PROGRESSIVE CHRISTIAN: If you wouldn't accept poison or disaster for your own, don't force it on strangers. Empathy is gospel, not a luxury. The Golden Rule draws the only real line, policy that protects only those behind your door is moral cowardice. If you wouldn't take disaster for your own kids, don't justify it for strangers. Empathy is the gospel, mandatory, not optional. The Golden Rule isn't just talk; it's the line that keeps society humane. If a policy only works because it spares you, it's not morality, it's pure cowardice.

4. Is this true to Jesus—or just theater?

> **CONSERVATIVE CHRISTIAN:** Reviving America means drawing hard lines and sticking to them. If truth upsets the crowd or sparks outrage, so be it because sometimes the culture needs shaking. Church isn't about applause. When the mob mocks, dig in.

> **PROGRESSIVE CHRISTIAN:** If Jesus walked in, would he see truth or just spin? Truth that can't handle scrutiny or the voices of the marginalized is a sham. Jesus went after the self-righteous, he didn't pander to donors or power. Real gospel wrecks comfort, risks honesty, and puts the struggling first. That's not theater; that's a revolution.

In the end, this isn't a contest for sounding the most spiritual or quoting the most Scripture. Both perspectives—claims, critiques, and consequences—are on display. What finally matters isn't who argued loudest, but which path draws us closer to the teachings and character of Jesus.

There are no perfect answers. This isn't about loyalty to a tribe, but about what kind of faith we're living: one that insulates us, or one that risks humility and love in public life. At the end of the day, that's the real Jesus Principle test and the answer will shape not just our opinions, but the legacy our faith leaves in a burning world.

FROM FIRE TO FLOOD: A NATION AT RISK

Here's the reality: for most Americans, climate change is no longer just a future threat because it has moved into the neighborhood. This isn't some distant headline:

- In New Jersey last July, flash floods turned highways into rivers and drowned subway stations, leaving families stranded for days, with at least two dead.[66]

- In Central Texas that same month, a hundred-year flood struck in the middle of the night, swamping homes as, unbelievably, the Guadalupe River jumped twenty-six feet in under an hour. There were at least 136 dead, including 37 children, and thousands were displaced.[67]

- In St. Louis this past spring, an EF–3 tornado flattened entire city blocks, most of them in neighborhoods where insurance is a luxury, not a guarantee. There were at least five dead, 38 injured, and over 10,000 properties damaged.[68]

- Over in New Mexico, survivors of last year's wildfires faced a second disaster as monsoon rains sent deadly debris flows tearing through already-devastated communities. There were at least three dead, including two children; hundreds

---

66. CNN, "More slow-moving storms move across a flood-weary East Coast, leaving at least two dead," July 14, 2025, https://www.cnn.com/2025/07/14/weather/flash-flood-threat-northeast-climate; BBC, "Two dead after flash flooding in New Jersey and New York City," July 15, 2025, https://www.bbc.com/news/articles/c0j42xy47q7o; USA Today, "Flash floods in NYC and the Mid-Atlantic; 2 killed in New Jersey," July 15, 2025, https://www.usatoday.com/story/news/weather/2025/07/15/flash-floods-new-york-city-mid-atlantic/85204068007/.

67. New York Times, "The Lives Lost to the Texas Floods," August 4, 2025, https://www.nytimes.com/interactive/2025/07/09/us/texas-floods-victims.html; Texas Tribune, "Texas Hill Country floods: What we know so far," July 11, 2025, https://www.texastribune.org/2025/07/11/texas-hill-country-floods-what-we-know/; Wikipedia, "July 2025 Central Texas floods," https://en.wikipedia.org/wiki/July_2025_Central_Texas_floods.

68. National Weather Service, "May 16 St. Louis and Des Arc Tornadoes," May 18, 2025, https://www.weather.gov/lsx/05_16_2025; St. Louis Public Radio, "A month after the tornado, St. Louisans begin to apply for aid to rebuild," June 15, 2025, https://www.stlpr.org/health-science-environment/2025-06–16/month-tornado-st-louisans-apply-aid-rebuild.

were displaced, adding to the 8,000 displaced by last year's wildfires.[69]

- The Los Angeles wildfires in January 2025 burned more than 57,000 acres across L.A. County, destroying more than 18,000 homes, schools, and businesses and forcing 200,000 residents to flee. At least 31 people were confirmed dead, with later estimates linking as many as 440 total deaths to smoke exposure and indirect health impacts. Insured losses topped $75 billion, total damage exceeded $250 billion, and neighborhoods from Malibu to Altadena were left in ashes—a searing reminder that the climate crisis is no longer coming; it's already here.

Entire neighborhoods don't know if their homes or jobs will survive the next storm. The impacts aren't equal; wealth buys security, while vulnerable groups—single moms, seniors, immigrants, Black, Hispanic, and Indigenous communities—stand most exposed and are too often forgotten when disaster hits.[70]

The church now faces a bigger test than worship or fundraising: will it defend those at risk, or turn away? Courageous compassion, not comfort or retreat, shaped Christianity's legacy. If climate is the

---

69. CNN, "Flash flood hits New Mexico mountain town, leaving at least 3 dead," July 8, 2025, https://www.cnn.com/2025/07/08/weather/new-mexico-ruidoso-flooding-hnk; The Gila Herald, "Three dead in New Mexico monsoon flooding," July 8, 2025, https://gilaherald.com/three-dead-in-new-mexico-monsoon-flooding/; Las Cruces Sun-News, "Three dead during historic flash flooding in Ruidoso," July 9, 2025, https://www.lcsun-news.com/story/news/local/2025/07/09/three-dead-during-historic-flash-flooding-in-ruidoso/84512645007/.

70. https://www.oxfamamerica.org/explore/issues/climate-action/climate-change-and-inequality/; World Bank, "Social Dimensions of Climate Change," https://www.worldbank.org/en/topic/social-dimensions-of-climate-change; Kaiser Family Foundation, "Understanding the Inequitable Impacts of Hurricanes and Other Natural Disasters," https://www.kff.org/racial-equity-and-health-policy/understanding-inequitable-impacts-hurricanes-other-natural-disasters-the-wake-hurricanes-helene-and-milton/.

new frontline, American Christianity must quickly choose a side. The coming decades will show whether the church is remembered for sacrificial love or empty rhetoric. The story is still being written.

WHAT TO TOSS, WHAT TO KEEP?

The next step is getting practical about what to toss aside, and what's truly worth keeping in a faith that faces a burning world head-on.

Toss out:

- End-times fatalism and spiritual escapism
- Dismissing climate suffering as "hype"
- Using "dominion" as a license to exploit creation

Keep:

- Humility: learning, admitting mistakes, changing direction
- Courage: speaking up for the vulnerable
- Practical action: restoration, protection, and creation care

Why?

- Dr. Jonathan Moo highlights that so-called "end-times fatalism," the claim that it's pointless to care for the earth because it will all end anyway, is spiritual escapism, not biblical Christianity. Faithfulness means staying engaged, not checking out.

- Dr. Katharine Hayhoe and other Christian ethicists (including the Lausanne Movement) warn that dismissing climate disasters as hype ignores our obligation to witness and respond compassionately to real suffering in our midst.

- A. J. Swoboda and the Evangelical Environmental Network argue that interpreting "dominion" as a license for exploitation distorts both Genesis and Jesus's model of service; true stewardship requires defending the powerless and honoring creation, not exploiting it.

BOTTOM LINE

A Jesus-shaped filter clears away slogans and spin, leaving a legacy of humility, courage, and concrete restorative action.

CONCLUSION: WRITING A NEW CHAPTER

Anna's questions are now the entire world's crisis. The sky she saw—red, smoky, and silent—isn't imagination but prophecy: science says we are on the very edge of climate tipping points. And once we pass that brink, there's no easy way—and maybe no way—back. This is not speculation. It's why so many climate scientists are experiencing climate anxiety, distress, and burnout: they see the storm coming and know it cannot be bargained with or voted away.

Today, ninety-seven percent of climate scientists from every nation and discipline agree: human-driven climate change is a fact, not a theory.[71] Tipping points—whether melting ice sheets, destroyed coral reefs, or runaway methane in the Arctic—are not ifs; they are whens. The first will arrive soon. Once triggered, changes cannot be undone, resulting in cascading disruptions that threaten food, water, homes, and millions of lives.

---

71. NASA, "Do scientists agree on climate change?" https://science.nasa.gov/climate-change/faq/do-scientists-agree-on-climate-change/; Skeptical Science, "The 97% consensus on global warming," https://skepticalscience.com/global-warming-scientific-consensus.htm; AAAS, "What We Know," https://whatweknow.aaas.org/index.html.

People on the margins—those Anna prayed for, and many she could never meet—are already paying the price. The world's most vulnerable are suffering mass loss of life, and every year the death toll grows. That's happening now. What begins with hundreds of thousands will become millions unless the story changes, and soon.

THERE IS ALWAYS HOPE ON THE HORIZON

Scientists do carry a gospel of hope: real action, taken now, can still rewrite our collective future. Solutions exist with aggressive carbon cuts, clean energy, restored forests, and frontline climate adaptation. Our youngest generation gets it—they're marching, organizing, acting—while the rest of us argue. The window for rescue may be narrow, but it's real.

Faith with courage, humility, and self-sacrifice has always been fierce enough to change even the hardest hearts and the toughest odds. This is one of those moments. If Christians, neighbors, and leaders of conscience rise-up—acting not tomorrow but now—Anna's story could belong to a generation that refused despair, chose mercy, and saw shelter as sacred. This crisis is not just about policy. It's life and death, and it's personal. The church's answer will shape whether history remembers bold hope—or another tragic silence—as the world caught fire.

May our grandchildren count us among those who did not flinch from danger, or from our duty to love, fiercely, when it mattered most.

CHAPTER 7

LGBTQ+ AND THE CHURCH

UNSEEN AND UNLOVED

She sat alone, clutching a crumpled letter from her parents: "We love you, but we can't accept this lifestyle." The words blurred behind her tears.

She'd prayed for years to change—attending church camps, begging God to "fix" her. But the shame never lifted. At school, classmates mocked her. At church, the pastor thundered that "same-sex attraction is a demonic lie."

As days grew heavier, she wondered if her parents would ever see her as anything but sin. In the hush of night, a fearful question surfaced: Has God abandoned me?

That night, she reached for a handful of pills.

This tragedy is not unique. Across America, countless LGBTQ+ youth face rejection and cruelty from the very families and churches meant to love them, turning homes and sanctuaries into crucibles of shame and despair.

WHAT'S THIS LGBTQ+ ALL ABOUT?

Before diving into the struggles of LGBTQ+ youth, let's clear up what those five letters and plus sign mean. Understanding a community starts with knowing who's in it:

- L: Lesbian, women who love women.
- G: Gay, usually men attracted to men, but sometimes an umbrella for anyone attracted to the same gender.
- B: Bisexual, attracted to more than one gender.
- T: Transgender, gender identity does not match sex assigned at birth.
- Q: Queer or Questioning, "Queer" is flexible for anyone outside the norm; "Questioning" means exploring identity.
- +: Plus: the wildcard for intersex, asexual, nonbinary, pansexual, genderfluid people, and lots more—it's the "and all the rest" of human experience.

The acronym has expanded to reflect the spectrum of real lives, with "+" ensuring inclusivity for all. Sexuality itself is not black or white. It's a rainbow spectrum, a gradient with infinite shades, shown by science across psychology, biology, and lived experience.

People's attractions and identities refuse to fit in neat boxes, and that is perfectly natural and human. But knowing who belongs under the LGBTQ+ umbrella is only the beginning, because every letter and label represents a real life, and too many, especially youth, have stories carved out by struggle, rejection, and heartbreak.

THE TRAGIC REALITY

The girl's story at the start isn't just personal heartbreak, it's a national crisis. Nearly forty percent of LGBTQ+ youth seriously consider suicide each year, with even higher rates among transgender and nonbinary youth. More than one in ten attempt, vastly outpacing national averages.[72] These aren't caused by being LGBTQ+ but by rejection, stigma, bullying, discrimination, family and church exclusion, and harmful policies.

LGBTQ+ youth are over twice as likely to face homelessness, often exiled by religious parents.[73] Research from Dr. Caitlin Ryan, Dr. Curtis J. VanderWaal, and journals like *Social Work & Christianity* confirm that religious rejection in conservative Christian homes sharply raises risks for isolation, depression, and abandonment, falling far short of the love of Jesus they claim to reflect.

These wounds run deepest in non-affirming faith communities, where being gay or trans is taught as wrong, and LGBTQ+ youth are denied full membership or leadership. Such environments make it especially difficult to feel truly safe or loved.

However, some conservative families and churches are pushing for more support—pastoral care, mental health assistance, harm

---

72. The Trevor Project, "2024 National Survey on LGBTQ+ Youth Mental Health," https://www.thetrevorproject.org/survey-2024/; CDC, "More than 40% of LGBTQ youth said they considered suicide in the past year, CDC report finds," https://abcnews.go.com/Health/40-lgbtq-youth-considered-suicide-past-year-cdc/story?id=112604907.

73. Caitlin Ryan, "Supportive Families, Healthy Children: Helping Families with Lesbian, Gay, Bisexual & Transgender Children," Family Acceptance Project, https://familyproject.sfsu.edu; Curtis J. VanderWaal, Adrienne B. Dessel et al., "LGBTQ Topics and Christianity in Social Work: Tackling the Tough Questions," Social Work & Christianity 44, no. 1 & 2 (2017): 11–30, https://www.nacsw.org/Publications/SWC/SWC44_1&2.pdf.

reduction—even without dropping their doctrines. Hearts do sometimes move faster than official positions.

Beneath the statistics are deeper fears and beliefs shaping not just policies but the everyday responses when youth come out.

FEAR, BLACK-AND-WHITE THINKING, AND THE MYTH OF CHOICE

Why do some Christian families and churches respond to LGBTQ+ youth with such staggering harshness and intolerance? For many conservative Christians, the debate over LGBTQ+ rights is viewed as a black-and-white, all-or-nothing issue. LGBTQ+ children are not seen as beloved sons and daughters made in the image of God but instead treated as contradictions to church teaching and sometimes labeled "abominations," with Leviticus 20:13 ominously hanging overhead: "If a man lies with a male as with a woman … they shall surely be put to death." These ancient words, still quoted by some, create a shadow of conditional love and potential erasure that haunts many LGBTQ+ youth in conservative Christian settings.

A pervasive fear underlies this rigid response: the idea that accepting LGBTQ+ people threatens the faith, the family, or community standards. Is this fear driven by love, or by insecurity and a need for control? Actions shaped by fear lead to zero-sum thinking: every move toward compassion or empathy for LGBTQ+ youth is seen by some as a slippery slope. Offering understanding or affirmation is viewed not as Christlike, but as a risk to doctrine or to family values.[74]

---

74. Clara L. Wilkins and Lerone A. Martin, "Research documents how fundamentalists view LGBTQ inclusion as a zero-sum game they are losing," Baptist News Global, September 6, 2021, https://baptistnews.com/article/research-documents-how-fundamentalists-view-lgbtq-inclusion-as-a-zero-sum-game-they-are-losing/; S. Davidai and M. Ongis, "Examining Christian/Sexual Orientation Zero-Sum Beliefs," Journal of Personality and Social Psychology, 2020, https://www.apa.org/pubs/journals/releases/psp-pspi0000363.pdf.

Most adults, let alone children and teens, cannot imagine the crushing burden of such brutal rejection. People who once offered encouragement—parents, teachers, clergy—now wield condemnation as a tool, meant as guidance, received as control. Sermons and lectures deliver ultimatums: "Change who you are or lose everything."

Consider Matthew Vines, raised in a conservative evangelical church in Kansas. When he came out as gay, his faith community rejected him, leaders declared his orientation incompatible with Christianity, and old friendships evaporated. The sense of loss and abandonment spiraled into depression and deep isolation. The message was clear: "You can be part of us, but only if you deny who you are."

Matthew's story, and those like his, are reminders that evangelical teachings—when applied rigidly and without compassion—risk turning faith into a vector of lasting wounds.

Is it any wonder LGBTQ+ youth ask if they'll ever be enough, or if love is even possible for them? For too many, the pain turns inward, breeding isolation, despair, and a hopelessness so deep that self-harm or even suicide appears as an escape. For some conservative religious parents, faith—often unintentionally—can become a source of pain or exile for their LGBTQ+ children.

CAN YOU BE GAY AND CHRISTIAN?

This question isn't just an abstract or academic debate, it's tearing entire denominations and families apart. Many Americans, even devout Christians, are surprised to learn that in some churches, the rainbow flag waves beside the cross, LGBTQ+ pastors preach from the pulpit, and same-sex couples are married at the altar. For those raised on "it's not possible," this reality shakes the foundation of inherited beliefs.

Consider the United Methodist Church (UMC), one of the nation's largest Protestant bodies. In 2024, the UMC lifted its ban on ordaining LGBTQ+ clergy and allowing same-sex marriages. This historic vote led thousands of conservative congregations to depart, forming the new Global Methodist Church and vowing to uphold the old bans. The split is the largest American denominational break since the Civil War, with echoes of previous church divides over slavery and women's rights.[75]

What does this schism really mean? At its core, it raises a piercing question: Does God exclude LGBTQ+ people, or does Jesus's teaching point to a greater welcome? Is inclusion faithfulness, or is it compromise? For affirming churches, sexual orientation is no barrier to faith or leadership. For non-affirming churches, embracing LGBTQ+ people is seen as a slide away from biblical clarity.

Yet, the real dilemma is not doctrine, but belonging: Is church a place for healing or for harm? Does clinging to tradition and exclusion move us closer to Jesus, or does it build a wall He would have torn down? Is a church truly Christlike if it tells anyone "Not you" at the door? Or is the truest test of faith how wide we are willing to draw the circle, and who we are willing to call "family"?

At the heart of this struggle are two very different readings of Scripture, each shaping not only theology but the daily realities of church life and policy.

---

[75]. NPR, "United Methodist Church lifts bans on LGBTQ clergy and same-sex weddings," May 1, 2024, https://www.npr.org/2024/05/01/1248468256/united-methodist-church-lifts-bans-on-lgbtq-clergy-and-same-sex-weddings; CNN, "United Methodist Church lifts 40-year ban on LGBTQ clergy," May 1, 2024, https://www.cnn.com/2024/05/01/us/united-methodist-church-lgbtq-clergy-reaj; PBS, "Methodist pastor discusses major shift in church over LGBTQ+ inclusion," May 16, 2024, https://www.pbs.org/newshour/show/methodist-pastor-discusses-major-shift-in-church-over-lgbtq-inclusion.

DUELING BIBLES: THE CONSERVATIVE CHRISTIAN PERSPECTIVE

For many conservative Christians, the Bible is seen as inerrant and unambiguous on sexuality, including same-sex relationships. Key leaders and organizations—Tony Perkins (Family Research Council), Franklin Graham (Samaritan's Purse), Kristen Waggoner (Alliance Defending Freedom), pastors John MacArthur (Grace Community Church, CA) and Paula White (Head of White House Faith Office)—shape this viewpoint publicly and politically.

The core biblical texts frequently cited include:

- Leviticus 20:13: "If a man lies with a male as with a woman, both of them have committed an abomination. They shall surely be put to death"—which, while no longer seen as a call for literal punishment, signals the seriousness with which same-sex relationships are viewed.

- Romans 1:26–27: "For this reason, God gave them up to vile passions. For their women changed the natural function into that which is against nature. Likewise, also the men, leaving the natural function of the woman, burned in their lust toward one another, men doing what is inappropriate with men, and receiving in themselves the due penalty of their error."

- 1 Corinthians 6:9–10: "Or don't you know that the unrighteous will not inherit God's Kingdom? Don't be deceived. Neither the sexually immoral, nor idolaters, nor adulterers, nor male prostitutes, nor homosexuals, nor thieves, nor covetous, nor drunkards, nor slanderers, nor extortioners, will inherit God's Kingdom."

- 1 Timothy 1:9–10: "As knowing this, that law is not made for a righteous person, but for the lawless and insubordinate, for the ungodly and sinners, for the unholy and profane, for murderers of fathers and murderers of mothers, for manslayers, for the sexually immoral, for homosexuals, for slave dealers, for liars, for perjurers, and for any other thing contrary to the sound doctrine."

IS EMPATHY GOOD OR BAD?

Recently, writers like Joe Rigney and Allie Beth Stuckey have criticized empathy as a danger to faith. Rigney's *The Sin of Empathy* argues that "untethered" empathy—defined as emotionally aligning with others without regard for biblical truth—can lead to emotional manipulation and undermine discernment in the church.[76] He distinguishes genuine compassion (rooted in moral clarity) from an empathy that caves to cultural and emotional pressure, sometimes linking these vulnerabilities with contemporary feminism and shifting gender roles.

Stuckey's *Toxic Empathy* echoes these concerns, warning that compassion divorced from scriptural standards can erode conviction and weaken church boundaries.[77] Both authors see empathy, when elevated above biblical authority, as a threat that could move churches away from steady principles and toward appeasement. They warn that calls for mercy may blur the lines necessary to protect orthodoxy and

---

76. Joe Rigney, *The Sin of Empathy: Compassion and Its Counterfeits* (Founders Press, 2025); see also Joe Rigney, interview by Albert Mohler, "The Sin of Empathy—A Conversation with Joe Rigney," February 18, 2025, https://albertmohler.com/2025/02/19/joe-rigney/.

77. Allie Beth Stuckey, discussion on "Toxic Empathy," Resurge with Josh Howerton & Josh McPherson, January 23, 2025, https://www.youtube.com/watch?v=EeaL0hji2gQ; Allie Beth Stuckey, "Wimpy Women's Ministries Are Making the Church Weak," March 30, 2025, https://www.youtube.com/watch?v=XZp05-z1Bgk.

order. Some even frame empathy as a feminine weakness that weakens doctrinal clarity and strong leadership.

Some critics of Rigney and Stuckey's work argue that redefining empathy in this way provides cover for ongoing exclusion and discrimination, simply by claiming one's "empathy" isn't what Jesus intended. With so much at stake—community, doctrine, culture, and family—many opt to protect established boundaries by narrowing or even warning against empathy itself.

PROJECT 2025, CHRISTIAN NATIONALISM, AND THE LEGISLATIVE ASSAULT

In America, beliefs shaped in church often drive action far beyond the pews, influencing laws and public policy. Recent years have seen a surge of anti-LGBTQ+ legislation, much of it linked to Project 2025, a coordinated Christian nationalist agenda aiming to roll back LGBTQ+ rights and define America as a nation where only one brand of faith and family truly "belongs." This movement threatens not just same-sex marriage, but basic protections in health care, employment, schools, and homes.[78]

Scapegoating minorities isn't new: after 9/11, conservative preachers blamed America's "acceptance of the gay lifestyle" for the tragedy, a message with no biblical foundation but plenty of political utility.[79]

---

78. Axios, "What Project 2025 could mean for LGBTQ+ Americans," November 6, 2024, https://www.axios.com/2024/11/07/project-2025-lgbtq-rights; GLAAD, "Project 2025 Exposed," June 22, 2025, https://glaad.org/project-2025/; Interfaith Alliance, "Project 2025 In Trump's First Month: The Threat to LGBTQ+ Rights and Freedoms," March 25, 2025, https://interfaithalliance.org/post/project-2025-in-trumps-first-month-the-threat-to-lgbtq-rights-and-freedoms.

79. Axios, "What Project 2025 could mean for LGBTQ+ Americans," November 6, 2024, https://www.axios.com/2024/11/07/project-2025-lgbtq-rights; GLAAD, "Project 2025 Exposed," June 22, 2025, https://glaad.org/project-2025/; Interfaith Alliance, "Project 2025 In Trump's First Month: The Threat to LGBTQ+ Rights and Freedoms," March 25, 2025, https://interfaithalliance.org/post/project-2025-in-trumps-first-month-the-threat-to-lgbtq-rights-and-freedoms.

As gay rights gained wider acceptance, targets shifted—especially to transgender people—fueled by fear and used as campaign weapons in the run-up to 2024.

Experts and advocacy groups warn that Project 2025 and broader Christian nationalist goals use fear and division to limit the rights of LGBTQ+ Americans and other minorities.[80] When fear becomes law, everyone's freedom is at risk, and defending dignity and equality becomes a responsibility that transcends any single faith or identity.

THE PROGRESSIVE AND MAINLINE CHRISTIAN PERSPECTIVE— THE CASE FOR GENEROUS EMPATHY

But there is another voice rising in the church, one that insists God's love is bigger than any doctrine of exclusion. Progressive Christians, mainline denominations, and a diverse group of organizations and leaders embody this perspective. Among them are Rev. Alba Onofrio at Soulforce, Bukola Landis-Aina at Q Christian Fellowship, David Thomas at Affirming Christian Fellowship, Marianne Duddy-Burke at DignityUSA, Jan Lawrence at Reconciling Ministries Network, Pastor Brandan J. Robertson at Missiongathering Christian Church in San Diego, and Sojourners.

They all point to the uncompromising welcome of Jesus, and their theological grounding is clear: Jesus consistently embraced those whom others put outside the circle, tax collectors, lepers, the ritually unclean.

---

80. GLAAD, "Project 2025 Exposed," June 22, 2025, https://glaad.org/project–2025/; Newsweek, "What Does Project 2025 Mean for the LGBTQ+ Community?" September 19, 2024, https://www.newsweek.com/what-does-project–2025-mean-lgbtq-people–1956315; Interfaith Alliance, "How Project 2025 Threatens Religious Freedom & Democracy," July 22, 2024, https://interfaithalliance.org/post/how-project–2025-threatens-religious-freedom-amp-democracy–2f854.

Mel White, Soulforce founder and former ghostwriter for Billy Graham and Jerry Falwell, summed up their conviction: "I'd rather suffer physical violence than be told by the church that my Creator doesn't love me as I am."[81] For these Christians, LGBTQ+ youth are not problems to be fixed, but beloved image-bearers of God, worthy of affirmation, dignity, and full inclusion.

To them, silence or complicity in the church is not just unfortunate, it's a refusal to "speak up for the vulnerable" (Proverbs 31:8–9). They ask: could the church become once again a sanctuary for those most at risk, truly embodying Jesus's habit of standing with society's outsiders?

These advocates urge churches not to settle for polite neutrality but to act with courage, affirming LGBTQ+ people in both teaching and practice, creating safe, welcoming space, and, just as Jesus did, siding with those whom tradition too often casts aside. Yet even in affirming communities, LGBTQ+ youth may still face challenges of identity, mental health, or acceptance, a reminder that affirmation, while necessary, is not itself a cure-all, but a foundation for deeper growth and inclusion.

THE JESUS PRINCIPLE AS A COMPASS

When the debate over LGBTQ+ identity and belonging burns hottest, the Jesus Principle as a compass asks a single question: Does this response move us toward the heart of Jesus, or away from it? The Gospels show Jesus consistently moved toward those on the margins, breaking social taboos, lifting those shamed by families and faith, and making room for the outcast at God's table. Not once did

---

81. Mel White, *Stranger at the Gate: To Be Gay and Christian in America* (Simon & Schuster, 1994); Mel White, "LGBT Resources," http://melwhite.org/lgbt-resources/.

he use difference as an excuse for rejection, and never did he teach that fear or exclusion honored God's love.

For Christians today, the Jesus-shaped compass doesn't settle for "love" that produces shame, despair, or loneliness. If doctrine or practice leaves LGBTQ+ youth despised or cast out, the direction is off course. The true north of Jesus points instead to radical compassion, dignity, and fierce solidarity with the vulnerable. Every choice—public and private—should be measured by whether it moves toward the embrace Christ gave to those society left behind.

THE JESUS PRINCIPLE AS A FILTER: WHAT TO TOSS, WHAT TO KEEP

A compass shows us direction, but a filter clears what poisons the well. The Jesus Principle as a filter pushes us to examine every doctrine, sermon, and tradition, and keep only what actually reflects the spirit and compassion of Jesus. We use four questions to help us discriminate toxins from the life-giving qualities that arise as we move towards the character and teachings of Jesus.

> **Author's Warning**: This isn't the part where anybody gets to play safe. Quoting Jesus isn't a magic spell that gives anyone the moral high ground. In fact, what comes next may draw blood because when the talk turns from slogans to lived consequences, "the way of Christ" won't let either side hide behind easy answers. If following Jesus costs nothing, you're probably doing it wrong. So, hold up both sides to the gospel-shaped mirror and brace for what comes next.

1. *Do these church rules bear the fruit of the Spirit—love, kindness, peace—or do they just deepen the pain of LGBTQ+ youth and families?*

   CONSERVATIVE CHRISTIAN: Biblical truth isn't about comfort. Sometimes love means drawing lines—even if it's called hate. If the church just wants to please people, it stops being a church. Calling sin what it is will always sting, but fake niceness that avoids truth is what really kills. Unity's worthless if it means selling out God for approval.

   PROGRESSIVE CHRISTIAN: If your faith leaves kids hurting or families split, it's not bearing fruit, it's doing damage. The measure isn't doctrine; it's how people are treated. If your gospel sends people away bleeding, it's not the Gospel. If your faith turns you into a weapon, it's time to check your fruit.

2. *Does your policy protect vulnerable kids—or shove them closer to suicide and despair?*

   CONSERVATIVE CHRISTIAN: Real faith means boundaries. If you throw open the doors to everything, you're not protecting the weak, you're inviting chaos. Charity isn't about blank checks; it's about hard limits. Don't call it "protection" if it puts the innocent at risk.

   PROGRESSIVE CHRISTIAN: If your rules push kids into the storm or make LGBTQ+ youth suicidal, that's not protection, it's neglect in disguise. If "caring for the vulnerable" means hurting the most vulnerable, your gospel's got nothing left. Jesus didn't build walls to keep the broken out.

3. *Would you want your own child or grandchild to be ostracized, shamed, or wounded by the same beliefs and rules you're defending?*

   Conservative Christian: Parenting and leading a church aren't about making people feel good. Sometimes love means tough truth, even when it hurts, even when they hate you for it. The courage to say "no" keeps people alive. Faith that never offends dies just to keep the peace.

   Progressive Christian: If you wouldn't want hell rained down on your child for being different, don't sign off on rules that do it to other people's kids. "Just following the Bible" isn't an excuse for cruelty. The Golden Rule isn't a suggestion: if this "truth" isn't good enough for your own family, it's not good enough for anyone else's. Don't pass off your comfort as God's will, put yourself in the firing line first.

4. *Is this response to LGBTQ+ people actually telling the truth like Jesus—or is it just theater for your comfort and control?*

   Conservative Christian: Strong words and boundaries aren't theater, they're what keep the church from becoming just another club. Jesus flipped tables; he didn't play nice for crowds. If conviction makes the world angry, maybe it means you're finally doing your job. Faith isn't applause.

   Progressive Christian: Jesus didn't play both sides, he broke the rules to heal and stood up for outcasts. That means something real: right now, almost forty percent of LGBTQ+ youth in conservative Christian homes are bullied, and one in ten seriously considers suicide. These kids aren't statistics; they're sons and daughters made in God's image, but too many are treated like problems to fix or threats to the family.

If your faith just builds a wall and leaves them to suffer, it's not faith—it's failure. Clean up your act: protect these kids, treat them as human, and remember if your gospel wouldn't let Jesus or your own child in the front door, it's not worth much. Lives are on the line.

THE JESUS PRINCIPLE AS A FILTER: WHAT TO TOSS, WHAT TO KEEP

The Jesus Principle as a filter pushes us to examine every doctrine, sermon, and tradition, and keep only what actually reflects the spirit and compassion of Jesus.

Toss out:

- Practices like conversion therapy, condemned as "torture" by the American Medical Association and rejected by the vast majority of mental health professionals
- Laws and sermons that build fear, shame, and division, and driving kids and adults from their homes, their faith, and their communities
- The claim that being LGBTQ+ is just a "choice" or that lawmakers, preachers, or families get to decide who's truly worthy of love and belonging
- Theologies arguing that empathy and compassion themselves are spiritual dangers, or that kindness is a slippery slope

Keep:

- A church, family, and community culture that puts the

vulnerable at the center, especially LGBTQ+ kids and teens pushed to the edge

- Empathy—the heart of Jesus's ministry—and policies that recognize the dignity and complexity of every person
- Safe, honest spaces for youth and families to wrestle with faith and identity, free from shame and coercion
- Active love: welcoming, affirming, and including, not just tolerating—and seeking justice wherever exclusion persists

BOTTOM LINE

If we filter out fear, shame, and exclusion, what's left is Jesus's own legacy: love, dignity, and hope, offered to every neighbor. That's the kind of faith, and the kind of church, worth fighting for.

REJECT DAMAGING DOCTRINE

If reading about LGBTQ+ realities in the church brings a realization that your beliefs or actions have done harm, don't start with blame, start with honest recognition. We all inherit doctrines shaped by tradition and culture, but even good intentions can cause lasting damage, as warned by major health and faith leaders. The point is not guilt but courage: a living faith grows by admitting when it's hurt the vulnerable and making it right.

Exodus International formally apologized for the harm caused by its "gay cure" ministries.[82] In 2024, Pope Francis publicly apologized

---

82. NPR, "Group That Claimed To 'Cure' Gays Disbands, Leader Apologizes," June 19, 2013, https://www.npr.org/2013/06/20/193965227/group-that-claimed-to-cure-gays-disbands-leader-apologizes; CBS News, "Pope Francis apologizes after being quoted using homophobic slur," May 28, 2024, https://www.cbsnews.com/news/pope-francis-apologizes-quoted-homophobic-slur/; Reuters, "Church of England apologises to LGBTQI+ people for 'shameful' treatment," January 20, 2023, https://www.reuters.com/world/uk/church-england-bishops-apologise-lgbtqi-people-2023-01-20/.

for using a homophobic slur and emphasized there is "room for everyone" in the church.[83] And in 2023, the Church of England's bishops issued an official apology to LGBTQ+ people for the church's history of exclusion and shame.[84]

The emerging consensus:

- Any boundary on membership or marriage must never excuse cruelty or ignoring suffering (Matthew 12:7, 1 John 4:20).
- Every person deserves to be treated as if Christ himself stood before us (Matthew 25:40, Luke 6:31, Matthew 7:12).
- The future of faith, families, and children depends on choosing justice, empathy, and love, rooted in Christ's own teaching (Micah 6:8, John 13:34, Zechariah 7:9–10).
- For every LGBTQ+ child, the church truly can become a place of hope, not harm (Matthew 19:14, Mark 9:42, John 10:10).

MOVING FORWARD

It's time to stop making excuses. Churches, families, and individuals can change the story by showing up with real welcome, fierce honesty, and the guts to protect their own—especially the LGBTQ+ kids whose lives hang in the balance.

Want to be like Jesus? No matter your religious doctrine, focus on treating your children like you would Jesus himself if he were among

---

83. CBS News, "Pope Francis apologizes after being quoted using homophobic slur," May 28, 2024.
84. Reuters, "Church of England apologises to LGBTQI+ people for 'shameful' treatment," January 20, 2023.

us today (Matthew 25:40). That means start by making your church safer than the world outside: build open tables, name stigma and stomp it flat, and let every child know they matter more than someone's quote from Leviticus.

Post your rules on the wall, talk mental health, and call out cruelty wherever it hides, but don't stop there. Trade in silence for hard conversations, build actual bridges, and let every outcast know their story won't end the way it started.

The girl in the opening vignette doesn't need platitudes or prayers behind closed doors, she needs safe spaces, bold action, and the kind of love that knocks down doors. The real Gospel means love gets loud and comfort stops being the goal.

CHAPTER 8

CHRISTIAN NATIONALISM

THE JESUS I MISS

She sits hunched in the last row, hiding in her oversized sweater as the teacher's prayer rolled through the classroom, loud, unbending, declaring that only one kind of Christianity belonged.

Doubt, here, was suspect.

Her stomach knotted. This faith felt sharp, almost brittle, a world away from the gentle Jesus she'd heard about at home.

At lunch, her Jewish friend leaned in, voice trembling: she didn't want to go back. Their Spanish-speaking classmate had vanished—papers, rumors, silence. The air between friends thickened, laughter replaced by glances at trays and muffled talk, fear choking honesty.

The warmth was gone. Every hush felt more like a warning than a welcome.

When did faith lose its kindness? She prayed in secret, not just for herself, but for her friends. Did God see them, even now?

Swallowing hard, she blinked away tears. She didn't want fear—in school or faith. She wanted to belong. To feel safe. To feel loved.

SETTING THE STAGE: CHRISTIAN NATIONALISM IN 2025

Let's cut through the noise: by autumn 2025, the conversation about conservative Christianity in America almost always circles back to its expanding role in politics, especially with nationalist language and faith-infused policies accelerating under President Trump's latest term. It's complicated, layered with contradictions, surprises, and everyday realities.[85]

But here's the twist: while media attention is roaring, these perspectives remain a minority. High-profile, yes, but not everyone's experience. Yes, Christian nationalism may grab headlines, but it's a vocal minority. Most believers want faith to shape hearts and homes, not write every law. Recognizing this gap matters, because it determines whose voices are amplified, and whose stories are left out.

PROJECT 2025

Project 2025, drafted by the Heritage Foundation and some hundred advocacy groups, has quickly moved from plan to policy by rolling

---

85. PBS, "Trump energizes conservative Christians with religious policies and assaults on cultural targets," August 7, 2025, https://www.pbs.org/newshour/politics/trump-energizes-conservative-christians-with-religious-policies-and-assaults-on-cultural-targets; Vox, "Donald Trump is building a strange, new religious movement," June 13, 2025, https://www.vox.com/politics/416042/religion-politics-trump-christian-nationalism-liberty-maga; CNN, "White Christian nationalists are poised to remake America in their image under another Trump term, scholar says," January 12, 2025, https://www.cnn.com/2025/01/12/us/white-christian-nationalism-du-mez-cec.

out hundreds of proposals, including expanded school vouchers and cuts to DEI programs. By late 2025, nearly half the agenda is now federal and state policy, often framed in biblical terms.[86]

The movement's roots reach back to Paul Weyrich, Jerry Falwell, Pat Robertson, Ralph Reed, and Heritage Foundation strategists fifty years ago, aiming to soften or erase barriers between church and state: eliminate the Department of Education, restrict abortion, and fund religious schools.[87]

But not all conservatives agree. Many support religious freedom for all, wary of clergy shaping every law. Some see this shift as moral renewal; others, even among conservatives, feel uneasy as pluralism seems threatened. The nation hovers, unsure where the line between faith and freedom should be drawn.

FROM BLUEPRINTS TO EVERYDAY IMPACT

As Project 2025 advances, anxiety and fear grow in communities that once felt secure. Federal and state agencies now enforce new policies and, in some cases, deploy ICE teams against protesters. Alarms rise as both immigrants and American citizens face detention or disappear from public view without due process and no access to lawyers.[88]

---

86. Wikipedia, "Project 2025," last modified August 28, 2023, https://en.wikipedia.org/wiki/Project_2025; Americans United, "Project 2025: A Christian Nationalist playbook outlines a broad scheme to overthrow American democracy and install a theocracy," June 9, 2024, https://www.au.org/the-latest/church-and-state/articles/destroying-life-and-liberty-a-christian-nationalist-playbook-outlines-a-broad-scheme-to-overthrow-american-democracy-and-install-a-theocracy/.

87. Wikipedia, "Christian right," last modified July 21, 2002, https://en.wikipedia.org/wiki/Christian_right; Talking Points Memo, "Brief History of the Christian Right," March 1, 2017, https://talkingpointsmemo.com/cafe/brief-history-of-the-christian-right.

88. Bridging Divides Initiative, "Issue Brief: Mapping the Rise in Immigration-Related Demonstrations in Early 2025," March 15, 2025; HIAS, "The ICE Raids — What You Need to Know," August 28, 2025; Harvard Law Review, "The Immigrant Rights Resistance Lives," April 22, 2025.

Supporters call this necessary for security, but watchdogs and faith leaders warn that it risks normalizing dangerous exceptions. The real debate isn't just about politics, it's about what matters more: safety, liberty, or dignity for all. In this tense moment, the moral compass behind policy decisions has never mattered more.

AT THE CROSSROADS: WHOSE BIBLE SETS THE COURSE?

Here's where the deeper conflict crystallizes. The real struggle comes down to which interpretation—especially for biblical literalists, whose version of biblical inerrancy—will ultimately call the shots for American public life, as Christians of all stripes wrestle with whose Bible sets the nation's moral direction.

This debate is more than politics; it's spiritual theater. Organizations like the New Apostolic Reformation frame it as a cosmic battle for America's soul: good vs. evil, Christian supremacy vs. pluralism. Leaders like Dutch Sheets, Charlie Shamp, Kenneth Copeland, and Lance Wallnau mobilize "spiritual warfare" and justify extreme measures by casting Trump as an instrument of divine purpose.[89]

Extremism flourishes in sharp binaries—us vs. them, sacred vs. secular—fracturing Christianity and deepening national division as biblical interpretation becomes a tool of public power.

---

89. Salon, "Meet the New Apostolic Reformation, cutting edge of the Christian right," January 1, 2024, https://www.salon.com/2024/01/02/meet-the-new-apostolic-reformation-cutting-edge-of-the-christian-right/; Religion News Service, "New Apostolic Reformation evangelicals see Trump as God's warrior in their battle to win America from satanic forces and Christianize it," November 10, 2024, https://religionnews.com/2024/11/11/new-apostolic-reformation-evangelicals-see-trump-as-gods-warrior-in-battle-to-christianize-america/.

DUELING BIBLES: THE CONSERVATIVE CHRISTIAN PERSPECTIVE

Conflicting convictions shape today's Christian landscape and spark debate between and within each camp. High-profile leaders associated with Christian nationalism—General Michael Flynn, Tony Perkins (Family Research Council), Kevin Roberts (Heritage Foundation), David Barton (WallBuilders), Paula White (White House Faith Office)—publicly push for government priorities aligned with their biblical traditions.

These leaders want public law based on their Christian values and not strict church-state separation. The verses they reference include:

- "Blessed is the nation whose God is Yahweh" (Psalm 33:12)

- "Let every soul be in subjection to the higher authorities …" (Romans 13:1)

- "If my people … will humble themselves, pray … then I will hear from heaven … and will heal their land" (2 Chronicles 7:14)

- "Go and make disciples of all nations … teaching them to observe all things that I have commanded you" (Matthew 28:19–20)

But pause here. Not every conservative Christian signs onto this movement or even sees it as true to their faith. In fact, there are influential dissenters within evangelical and conservative circles that have sounded alarms about conflating Christian faith with national identity. These include Russell Moore, former head of the Southern Baptist Convention's Ethics & Religious Liberty Commission; Beth

Moore, prolific author and Bible study leader who founded Living Proof Ministries; and David French, evangelical conservative writer, constitutional lawyer, and author.[90]

Across conservative and mainline Christianity, you'll find voices like these raising red flags about blending gospel and government. These aren't your typical liberal critics; they're pastors, theologians, and longtime Republicans who worry that we're heading down a dangerous path. They've read the history books; they know what happens when political power and religious authority get too cozy.

What's encouraging? There's a quieter groundswell happening, conservative evangelicals teaming up with mainline Protestants, Catholics joining hands with Methodists, all working together on joint statements and coalitions. Their mission? Protecting religious freedom for everyone, not just some Christians. Defending pluralism. Calling for civil dialogue instead of culture war battles.[91]

Their message cuts straight to the heart: The family of faith is diverse, and real collaboration becomes possible when humility and core ethical commitments take the lead over partisan politics.

---

90. Religion News Service, "David French on Christian nationalism and evangelicals' existential angst," February 2, 2021, https://religionnews.com/2021/02/03/david-french-on-christian-nationalism-and-americas-existential-angst/; ChurchLeaders, "Beth Moore's Tweet on Christian Nationalism Goes Viral," November 14, 2022, https://churchleaders.com/news/438751-beth-moores-tweet-on-christian-nationalism-goes-viral.html; The New Yorker, "The Theologian Russell Moore on Christian Nationalism," November 7, 2022, https://www.newyorker.com/podcast/politics-and-more/the-theologian-russell-moore-on-christian-nationalism.

91. Interfaith America, "How to Build Democracy Coalitions to Meet this Moment," June 22, 2025, https://www.interfaithamerica.org/article/how-to-build-democracy-coalitions-to-meet-this-moment/; Berkley Center, Georgetown University, "Too Few Faiths in a Nation of Many," August 21, 2025, https://berkleycenter.georgetown.edu/responses/too-few-faiths-in-a-nation-of-many.

THE PROGRESSIVE AND MAINLINE CHRISTIAN PERSPECTIVE

Look across the aisle—or even just down the pews—and a different approach comes into view. Progressive and mainline Christians, including a name that is self-explanatory: Christians Against Christian Nationalism—led by the Baptist Joint Committee for Religious Liberty and its executive director, Amanda Tyler—and thought leaders such as Brian McLaren of the Center for Action and Contemplation, are sounding the alarm based on their reading of Scripture:

- "My Kingdom is not of this world," Jesus insists (John 18:36)
- "Give … to Caesar the things that are Caesar's, and to God the things that are God's" (Matthew 22:21)
- "You shall worship the Lord your God, and you shall serve him only" (Luke 4:5–8)
- "There is neither Jew nor Greek … slave nor free man … male nor female, for you are all one in Christ Jesus" (Galatians 3:28)

For these congregations, the Gospel calls people first and always to humility, justice, and fierce inclusion. They remind us that the early church grew not by seizing the reins of power, but as a minority movement: small, countercultural, often on the margins or under pressure. They argue that when faith becomes a tool for dominance, it loses what makes it sacred.[92]

So, what's a reader—Christian, skeptic, or in-between—to do amid such parallel and passionately held convictions? Enter the Jesus

---

92. Ian Paul, "Racial, ethnic, and social diversity in the early church," Psephizo, April 7, 2024; The Master's University, "The Early Church's Example," June 1, 2025; Marks, "The Local Church as a Counterculture," May 20, 2025.

Principle. It's offered here as a practical lens, a four-question filter for navigating the tensions: a spiritual, ethical, and public compass meant to guide not only those who claim the faith but anyone seeking wisdom and integrity in a divided age.

THE JESUS PRINCIPLE AS A COMPASS

When the debate over faith in public life hits maximum turbulence, the Jesus Principle isn't just a gentle guide, it's a fierce compass demanding a gut check. Forget political talking points and churchy platitudes: the only question that matters now is whether Christian nationalism and its partisan approach to politics and religious belief moves us toward the real heart of Jesus or away from it.

If the result is shame, exclusion, fear, or cruelty—stop. The right direction is always deep-seated compassion, fierce protection of the vulnerable, and a willingness to rip down walls that keep anyone out. When convictions collide and "truth" gets weaponized, the Jesus Principle doesn't whisper, it points like true north to the embrace Christ gave outsiders. Every decision must face the fire: does this look like Jesus, or is it just theater?

How you answer these questions is strictly between you and God—no pastor, partner, or public opinion gets a vote. This is your conscience, your moment. Be real and true to yourself.

THE JESUS PRINCIPLE AS A FILTER

A compass gives direction; a filter demands clarity. The Jesus Principle presses every law, policy, and action through four clarifying questions: no hiding behind slogans or tribal comfort. In today's faith-fueled chaos, these questions cut through the noise and force genuine accountability.

Believers clash, politicians spin, but the test is direct: Does this bear the spirit of Jesus, protect the vulnerable, stand up for truth, no matter the cost? People will respond in very different ways, but each answer exposes the core values, beliefs, and priorities that drive them with nothing hidden and everything on the line. No easy outs, no shortcuts: move toward Christ's fierce compassion, or own the consequences. The verdict lands between the reader, their conscience, and God.

1. Does this political faith actually bear the fruit of the Spirit— or just stir up outrage and fear?

CONSERVATIVE CHRISTIAN: Strong faith means strong leaders and bold stances, even if passion is mistaken for anger. Courage is the real fruit: standing firm against a compromising culture. "Turn the other cheek"? That's for private life, not America's battles. When the nation is threatened, gentleness is weakness. Souls aren't won with soft words, but with conviction and power.

PROGRESSIVE CHRISTIAN: If your movement breeds outrage, fear, and exclusion, don't call it the fruit of the Spirit—call it toxic. Angry faith isn't holy just because it quotes Bible verses. When prayer turns political and faith divides instead of heals, you've traded the Gospel for a club. Christ's true Spirit is shown in compassion, open doors, and love for the least. The "fruit" you're producing is what's rotting the church.

2. Does this law, policy, or doctrine truly protect the vulnerable—or punish those who are already at risk?

CONSERVATIVE CHRISTIAN: God helps those who help themselves. We defend family, the unborn, and faith in schools. Borders exist for a reason; help starts and ends with citizens. If protecting "the vulnerable" means compromising laws or values, it's too high a cost. Strength and discipline matter most; let mercy follow order, not chaos.

PROGRESSIVE CHRISTIAN: This position is blunt: Jesus broke the rules for the sake of the vulnerable, end of story. "Order" that leaves the poor, immigrant, or excluded to suffer fails the Gospel test. When policies cause children's deaths, whose example is being followed: Christ or Caesar? The Gospel calls for solidarity, not just charity. If your movement builds walls and locks the gates, you side with the powerful, not the weak. Don't just talk about Christian values, show them through action.

3. Would I want this version of "truth" or "righteousness" forced on myself or those I love?

CONSERVATIVE CHRISTIAN: If the truth offends, good. A moral nation upholds standards, and real faith means demanding allegiance. If you're uncomfortable, change or push back. We won't apologize for legislating righteousness; if we don't shape law, someone else will. Sometimes the only way to save a culture is with tough love, even if that means discomfort for the few. Patriots make sacrifices; so should dissenters.

PROGRESSIVE CHRISTIAN: You want to force faith? Imagine your child questioned for their prayers, deported over paperwork, or denied care for loving the wrong person. That is what your "righteous laws" mean for the outcast. The Golden Rule isn't strategy, it's command. If you wouldn't accept forced belief for your family, don't inflict it on others. Jesus never coerced, he invited and lifted; forced faith is counterfeit.

4. Is this really faithful to Jesus—the truth at the center of the Gospel—or just a façade to maintain power?

> CONSERVATIVE CHRISTIAN: America used to stand tall as a city on a hill, founded on biblical truth. When history gets sanitized by "woke" revisionists, you lose your bearings. Our fight is to restore truth—God's truth—to the center. If uncomfortable facts are ignored, that's the cost of protecting national purpose. You don't preserve heritage by apologizing for it; you honor it by championing God's law, even if critics call it mythmaking.

> PROGRESSIVE CHRISTIAN: Truth is love, not propaganda. If your history cuts inconvenient facts, invents "Christian founders," or justifies injustice, you are no different than the Pharisees Jesus condemned. Power is not holiness. Admitting failure is difficult, but it's faith. If your "truth" can't survive honesty or the hard questions, it was never Christ's to begin with.

DISCERNMENT GETS URGENT

Jesus makes it plain: how we treat the poor, the sick, and the outsider is how we treat Jesus himself (Matthew 25:40). That's the core standard. Everything else is background noise.

When policies like those championed by Project 2025—restricted voting access, targeted action against immigrants, rollbacks on minority rights—take center stage, the question gets urgent. Are these actions about true protection, or do they quietly redraw the boundaries of who belongs? Do they show compassion, or create ever-sharper lines between "us" and "them"?

The USAID crisis is the perfect case study. In early 2025, the U.S. abruptly paused almost all foreign development aid, citing a review for "efficiency" and "accountability." Critics pointed out that

USAID's work has long been entangled with U.S. foreign policy interests, sometimes even supporting favored regimes alongside CIA intelligence efforts. Supporters argued that reforms require tough choices and that humanitarian aid can't be separated from global politics.

But the pause brought stark consequences: over 300,000 deaths worldwide, including more than 200,000 children, have been linked directly to the freeze. Proponents maintain that hard steps were essential to fix what was broken. Opponents counter with haunting clarity: what good is accountability if it means starving the world's most vulnerable?[93]

On the ground, the moral challenge becomes unavoidable. Families are denied food. Medical workers don't have supplies. Aid organizations have nowhere to turn. The Christian dilemma stares us in the face: are our political choices helping our neighbors, or forcing them to suffer so we can avoid responsibility for their pain?

SOUL SEARCHING TIME

This kind of evidence—documented by independent studies and reported in major media—demands soul-searching from any Christian serious about the Gospel's challenge. Making policy in the name of faith sounds noble, but when the consequences become heartbreakingly real, our true priorities get exposed. And it's never as simple as "one Christian view" because debate rages among conservatives, evangelicals, progressives, centrists, and across every denomination.

Moments like these press home the lesson: discernment isn't just about pure motives. History teaches us to look deeper, to use a sharper filter, probing beyond policies to the underlying legacies of race, power,

---

93. UN Human Rights Office of the High Commissioner, "US Government fuelling global humanitarian catastrophe: UN experts," July 30, 2025.

and exclusion that shape American Christianity. If the moral compass is about direction, the Jesus Principle's filter is about discernment, asking us to measure not only what we do today but how those choices echo through the past and into the future.

Nowhere does this filter feel more urgent—or more uncomfortable—than with race.

THE RACIAL RECKONING WE CAN'T AVOID

In America, faith and race aren't just tangled at the edges. For generations, white supremacy didn't thrive on the fringe but at the heart of church activism and politics, especially during civil rights battles. Robert P. Jones, in *White Too Long*, lays it bare: white Christian complicity wasn't an accident; it shaped beliefs, missions, and pulpits across time.[94]

Critics point out that the initial mobilization behind "religious liberty" frequently coincided with opposition to school integration and civil rights, a shield for existing power. Yet many inside these movements saw themselves defending faith and moral order amidst rapid change. That tension—motives and meaning, fear and faith—remains.

Today, studies routinely show that about two-thirds of white evangelicals identify with Christian nationalist thinking in some way.[95] But let's be honest: these are messy categories, debated not just between left and right but within conservative circles too. Neither leaders nor followers fit neatly on a spreadsheet, and the diversity inside every label deserves recognition.

---

94. Robert P. Jones, *White Too Long: The Legacy of White Supremacy in American Christianity* (New York: Simon & Schuster, 2020).
95. PRRI, "Christian Nationalism Across All 50 States: Insights from PRRI's 2024 American Values Atlas," July 1, 2025.

Here's what Jones doesn't ask for: endless blame. He calls for honest reckoning. That's how churches, and a nation, can finally reach for the integrity at the core of both democracy and faith. Across denominations, more voices are insisting that unflinching truth and genuine repentance are what make redemption possible, giving American Christianity the courage to confront, not simply relive, the old sins of racial injustice.

HISTORY DOESN'T WHISPER—IT SHOUTS

Let's be blunt: whenever church and state have merged, the fallout has been predictable: corruption, lost freedoms, and the gradual grinding down of conscience. Roger Williams, Thomas Jefferson, and James Madison knew this. Their "wall of separation" wasn't built to keep faith out, but to keep liberty in and to protect every soul's right to believe or not believe without political interference.

Today, we're seeing real-world results when pieces of conservative Christianity cozy up to power. The closer faith gets to the political flame, the more people step away. Church pews are emptier than they've been in generations, especially among those under forty. The Southern Baptist Convention has shed 3.5 million members since 2006, with about half that loss occurring during its most public political engagement with the Republican Party and Trump.[96] Meanwhile, the "nones"—those opting out of religious identity—are surging.[97]

What's the lesson? Tying Christianity to partisan power pushes away folks looking for spiritual belonging and turns a gospel of service into a vehicle for culture war. In the eyes of many under thirty,

---

96. Baptist News, "SBC membership shrank by nearly one-fourth in two decades," May 1, 2025.
97. Pew Research Center, "Decline of Christianity in the U.S. Has Slowed, May Have Leveled Off," February 25, 2025.

"evangelical" doesn't signal good news, it's code for conflict, division, and strife. The original message of radical welcome gets drowned out by political noise.

When politics take the pulpit, the pews start to empty.

THE JESUS PRINCIPLE AS A FILTER: WHAT TO TOSS, WHAT TO KEEP

A filter clarifies what belongs in a Jesus-shaped faith and what poisons the well, especially when politics and Christianity collide.

Toss out:
- Policies and rhetoric that demonize outsiders or equate dissent with danger
- Laws or religious interpretations that punish, repress, or exclude in Jesus's name
- The blending of faith and power that prioritizes winning over serving
- Historical revisionism or narratives that justify injustice for "God's" sake

Keep:
- Dignity for every neighbor, regardless of belief, background, or status
- Public life marked by practical compassion, mercy, and truth-telling
- A faith that protects the vulnerable, even at a political cost
- Humility, hospitality, and honest reckoning with both the past and present

BOTTOM LINE

True strength lies in faith that loves fiercely and acts justly, never using Jesus to build walls or justify domination. The more a policy looks like mercy, the closer it lands to the Jesus Principle.

Run any enforced faith through the Jesus Principle's filter, and the message from history is crystal clear: whenever a one-size-fits-all creed takes root, violence and division aren't far behind. Religion reduced to hollow ritual loses its pulse and its purpose.

These aren't academic warnings. Remember the nativist movements, or the Ku Klux Klan twisting "Christian nation" language into a weapon of exclusion and terror? Conservative Christians today acknowledge these as cautionary tales, not badges of honor. Fast forward to January 6 where scholars like Ruth Ben-Ghiat see the danger when democratic norms serve religious agendas.[98] The unraveling can be fast, and the damage stubbornly deep. Economist Umair Haque warns that when ideology overrides basic civic trust, economies shiver, inequality grows, and hope shrinks for everyone, not just the vulnerable.[99]

So at every major fork—national or personal—the Jesus Principle isn't just a compass for abstract values. It's a test for real life. Does this move us closer to Jesus's model of love, justice, and truth? Or does it leave us with fear, exclusion, and self-righteous certainty?

When we look closely, if what remains is division instead of reconciliation, that's our sign to pause and recalibrate. The filter isn't about tradition for tradition's sake because it must show its work in today's lived experience.

Armed with stories from the past and debates still echoing today, now's the time to ask hard questions of conviction, compassion, and

---

98. Ruth Ben-Ghiat, *Strongmen: Mussolini to the Present* (W. W. Norton & Company, 2020).

99. Umair Haque, "Eudaimonia & Co," https://eand.co (accessed September 2025).

the direction we're headed. The Jesus Principle demands it, and so does the world we're building together.

QUESTIONS FOR YOUR SOUL

As public and private beliefs get tested in real time, here are the hard questions you need to ask yourself:

- Is there fear, pride, or a desire to control lurking beneath this creed?
- Does the result lead toward inclusion or exclusion, hospitality or coercion?
- Are lessons from history guiding humility, or are we repeating old mistakes?
- After honest self-examination, does this teaching multiply compassion and freedom, or leave only division and zealotry?

What endures should align with both Scripture and the Jesus who embraces, restores, and makes room for everyone, including those at the center and those pushed to the margins.

As these questions linger, remember that even amid division and doubt, possibility survives. The next step isn't just intellectual, it's a lived commitment that honors the sacrifices of the past while reaching for a more compassionate, inclusive future.

HOPE LIVES HERE

Democracy isn't an abstraction. Lose it, and you lose the freedom to speak, pray, vote, or protest. Lately, rights for women, protesters, and dissenters are under attack. Fear is rising, and basic freedoms feel fragile. America's story isn't done. The only thing preserving hope? Ordinary people who show up, vote, challenge injustice, and refuse silence. These freedoms weren't gifts; they were fought for. It's on us now to protect and expand them—period.

FAITH AS RESISTANCE

Mainstream and progressive faith groups are fighting for democracy, not just their own rights but those of minorities and dissenters. True faith defends the vulnerable and challenges injustice, not just from the pulpit but in the public square. Leaders across traditions are standing against policies that exclude, pushing for compassion, justice, and authentic freedom for all. Faith means putting yourself on the line, so nobody gets shut out, no matter their background.

PERSONAL STAKES

On a personal note, this legacy is tangible for me. My father, Carl Johnson, served in the U.S. Army through the hardest days of World War II, facing peril in both European and Pacific theaters. Even though he was a staunch Republican, he didn't fight for one party or creed, but for an America where liberty endures even when challenged.

Honoring him means embracing hope over cynicism, refusing easy answers, and rejecting ideologies that close doors. It's a daily commitment: choose hope, welcome dialogue, and build a democracy that makes space for all faiths and every person.

CHOOSING HOPE

This all circles back to the girl sitting in the last row, hoping for kindness, praying her school and church would see her, not shame her. Her longing for safety, for a faith that felt like home, is the real test, and it always has been. When the church forgets the heart of Jesus, real people suffer.

Hope isn't sentimental; it's survival. Division, apathy, and power games aren't abstractions; they're bricks in a wall shutting out a new generation. Democracy won't defend itself. Faith can't mean much if it's just another word for party loyalty. When Christians trade the radical welcome of Jesus for the tribal comfort of culture wars, they lose the plot, and they lose their children.

Here's the blunt truth: The point of evangelical faith is the Good News, the Great Commission to make disciples, bringing hope, healing, and new life to every corner, every outsider, every culture. But if the Great Commission means moving into every culture, how can it be fulfilled when the focus shifts to culture wars that divide *us* versus *them*, walling off outsiders and turning a movement of welcome into a fortress of exclusion?[100]

Somewhere along the highway into politics, many have left the Great Commission at the off-ramp. In the hunger for power, the church is hemorrhaging its young. American Christianity is on pace to lose, if not an entire generation, then a good portion of it, and not because the Gospel failed, but because it got replaced by a ballot box, a bullhorn, and culture wars that are tearing the nation—and Christianity—apart.

There's a punchline no preacher wants: The more Christians move into politics, the more they seem to be moving out of church. It's a trade: more seats at the political table, fewer in the pews.

It's not just democracy that's on the line. The witness and future of Christian faith in America hang in the balance as long as culture

---

100. Lausanne Movement, "The Great Commission: A Theological Basis," May 23, 2024.

wars matter more than the Great Commission. If the movement keeps swapping grace for grievance, the hollow sound left in empty sanctuaries will tell the real story.

Now is the time for courage and honesty, and to choose hope with eyes wide open, stepping away from power plays and back toward the Jesus who started it all. The Good News was never "us versus them." It's always been "all are welcome," and that's the only message that has the power to last.

CHAPTER 9

A NEW PARADIGM

MARCUS AT THE CROSSROADS

Marcus sat in his truck outside First Baptist, watching familiar faces stream into the building he'd called home for fifteen years. These were the families who'd celebrated his highs, comforted his lows.

Now everything felt wrong.

Three weeks earlier, a simple question had changed everything. Troubled by the pastor's talk of immigrants as "threats," Marcus asked, "Shouldn't we ask what Jesus would actually do with families seeking help?" The silence in response spoke volumes.

Word spread. Invitations dried up. His Sunday school class became a minefield, with every comment judged by politics, not Scripture.

This morning, Marcus had to choose: Blend in, keep quiet, and keep his place. Or risk everything to follow the Jesus who broke bread with outsiders, defended the vulnerable, and said love was the only commandment that mattered.

His hand paused on the church door. What if following Jesus meant losing everything he'd ever called Christianity? What if the choice wasn't faith versus rebellion, but comfort versus honesty?

The sunlight hit stained glass across the parking lot. Safe. Familiar. But Marcus finally saw the danger of choosing safety over truth.

WE'RE ALL MARCUS NOW

Marcus's crisis is America's crisis. We're all standing at the same crossroads, staring at the same choice: Will we choose the Jesus we've inherited, or the Jesus we discover when we actually read what he said and did?

Will we follow the comfortable Jesus who blesses our politics and validates our prejudices? Or will we risk everything for the Jesus who ate with tax collectors, defended the accused woman, and told the rich young ruler that following him meant giving away everything? The stakes couldn't be higher. Not just for American Christianity, but for American democracy itself.

Marcus's crossroads isn't just a personal drama; it's the battleground for the soul of American Christianity. The Great Commission calls believers to bring hope to every outsider, every culture, and every community, expanding the circle of welcome. But when faith gets reduced to culture wars, the focus shifts from "Go to all nations" to "Protect our own." Outsiders become threats, not neighbors; mission turns to maintenance; the church trades away the Gospel's open invitation for a defensive posture that shuts people out and deepens division.

This is what's lost at this intersection: the entire purpose of Christian witness, moving toward the margins, not just patrolling the borders. Every time exclusion wins, faith shrinks to a banner waving over a fortress, and the world sees Christians more eager to fight than to invite. If Christianity forgets that its mission is invitation—not gatekeeping—the cost isn't just lost souls, but a lost future.

THE JESUS PRINCIPLE: YOUR FOUR QUESTIONS

You've read the arguments. You've seen the dueling Bibles. You've watched Christians use the same Scripture to justify opposite positions on everything from healthcare to immigration, from women's rights to LGBTQ+ dignity.

So how do you cut through the noise? How do you find your way when everyone claims to speak for God?

The Jesus Principle gives you four simple questions. Not to end the debate, but to ground you in something deeper than politics or tribe:

- **Am I bearing the fruit of the Spirit?** Love, joy, peace, patience, kindness, goodness, faithfulness, gentleness, self-control. If your faith produces anger, division, or exclusion, something's wrong.

- **Am I caring for the vulnerable?** Jesus said how we treat the poor, the sick, the stranger is how we treat him. Full stop.

- **Am I treating others as I want to be treated?** The Golden Rule isn't a suggestion. It's the measuring stick.

- **Am I committed to truth, even when it hurts?** Jesus didn't avoid uncomfortable realities. Neither should we.

These aren't theology questions. They're life questions. They're the compass that helps direct us and the filter that separates authentic faith from its many counterfeits. That's the power of the Jesus Principle, and why these four questions matter. Every time they're put into practice, they rip down the fences of exclusion and redraw the boundaries of grace.

When followers of Jesus use this filter, the old barriers—race, politics, status, fear—are exposed for the counterfeits they are. It's not just a personal test; it's the blueprint for a faith that refuses to shut out outsiders or shrink the circle. The answer isn't culture war, it's organic welcome: faith lived out so that every neighbor knows they actually belong. If the church wants to reclaim the heart of Jesus, this is how it starts: all are welcome, no exceptions.

THE COST OF FOLLOWING

Here's what nobody tells you about the Jesus Principle: it's expensive. It costs you the comfort of certainty, the safety of belonging, and the luxury of judging others while excusing yourself. It asks you to love people you've been taught to fear, to welcome those you've been told to exclude, to question beliefs you've never questioned before.

It might cost you friends who can't understand why you don't like the people they like or hate the ones they hate. It might cost you family members who think you've lost your way. It might even cost you your church, if your church has forgotten that the Gospel is good news for everyone, not just the people who look and think like you.

But here's what it gives back: integrity. Peace with yourself. The ability to look in the mirror and know that your faith is actually about following Jesus, not just wearing his name like a team jersey.

Don't kid yourself: settling for comfort is a great way to lose everything that matters. Christianity isn't supposed to feel safe. The real cost of picking comfort—or sticking with the crowd—is a shrinking soul, a faith that means less with each compromise, and a church full of people who never risk a thing and never change the world. "God can handle your doubts" is true, but it's not an excuse to never question, never grow, and never get uncomfortable.

Comfort is the enemy of conviction. If Christians keep soothing themselves with platitudes, the movement dies, slowly, quietly, and nobody will mourn its passing but the folks inside the bubble.

The risk of authenticity is steep: lost friendships, lost status, maybe even lost church. But the risk of staying comfortable is steeper: losing integrity, losing your way, and losing the call of Jesus entirely. That's not just a cost. It's a crisis. Faith without change ends up as nothing but nostalgia and noise.

THE CHOICE BEFORE AMERICA

We're not just choosing between political parties or policy positions. We're choosing between two completely different visions of what America can be:

- One vision is about power: who has it, who keeps it, who uses it to control others. It's about building walls, creating enemies, and making sure the "right" people stay on top. It uses the language of faith, but its fruits are fear, division, and exclusion.

- The other vision is about possibility: what happens when we actually try to love our neighbors as ourselves, when we build bridges instead of walls, when we measure our success by how we treat the most vulnerable among us.

The first vision leads to a Christian nation where only certain Christians are welcome. The second leads to a nation where Christians—and everyone else—can flourish together.

YOUR MOVE

This isn't a book designed to convert you to my politics or my theology. It's designed to help you live yours with integrity. Take the Jesus Principle home with you. Test it. Try it on the issues that matter most. See if it leads you closer to the heart of the Jesus you claim to follow, or further away. The Jesus Principle is doctrine-neutral, it works in any church or denomination, from Baptist to Lutheran to Catholic. No matter your tradition, test these questions honestly and see how they shape your faith in practice.

If you find it leads you away from positions you've held, don't panic. Course corrections aren't failures; they're signs of growth. The disciples got things wrong constantly. Peter denied Jesus three times. Paul spent years persecuting Christians before he became one.

God is big enough to handle your doubts, your questions, your changes of heart. What God can't handle is indifference, cruelty dressed up as righteousness, or love that stops at the border of our own tribe.

THE INVITATION

As former mega-church pastor Jim Palmer argues in *Inner Anarchist*, Jesus was an anarchist in the truest sense; not someone who destroys for destruction's sake, but someone who dismantles broken systems to build something better.[101] Jesus didn't come to start a religion. He

---

101. Jim Palmer, *Inner Anarchy: Dethroning God and Jesus to Save Ourselves and the World* (Jim Palmer, 2013).

came to start a revolution, a revolution of love that turns the world upside down, where the last become first, the weak become strong, and the outcasts become family.

That revolution is still happening. The question is whether you'll join it. Not the sanitized, politicized, weaponized version that calls itself Christianity while ignoring everything Jesus actually said and did. But the real thing. The dangerous thing. The thing that changes everything.

The choice is yours. It always has been.

Marcus chose. That morning in the church parking lot, he turned off the engine and walked away, not from faith, but toward it. Three months later, he and his family found a small Methodist church that sponsors refugee families and runs a weekend food pantry. Marcus volunteers every Saturday, using his agricultural background to help new immigrants learn about farming in America.

He lost some friendships. His old Sunday school class stopped inviting him to their monthly dinners. A few family members think he's gone "woke." But Marcus has never felt more at peace.

"I finally feel like I'm following Jesus instead of just talking about him," he told me last week. "My life got smaller in some ways, less certainty, fewer people who agree with me about everything. But it got bigger in the ways that matter. More love. More purpose. More peace."

Marcus stopped trying to defend Christianity and started living it.

YOUR TURN

Let's be blunt: the Jesus Principle isn't a sentimental slogan. It's a test of courage, not comfort. It doesn't care how long someone's been in a pew or how many Bible verses they can quote. It asks only this: will you follow the real Jesus, even when it costs you? Will you trade certainty and safety for integrity and costly love? Or will you settle for a faith that just fits in, plays it safe, and chooses political sides over the Gospel's demands?

This isn't academic. Lives are on the line. The reputation of Christianity, and the future of American democracy, stand in the balance. Churches will keep emptying as long as exclusion trumps love and politics replaces the Great Commission. The world—outsiders, doubters, and the next generation—is watching to see if Christians really mean what they say.

So, here's the choice, stripped of all platitudes: Will you pick the safety of the crowd, or the risk of actually following the Jesus of the Gospels? Will faith be another tribal badge, or will it be a revolution of love, mercy, and justice that wounds pride but heals the world?

It's your move. No more hiding behind slogans, no more blaming others for what Christians have become. This is the moment—maybe the last clear one for a while, at least in the United States—to walk out of the parking lot and follow, all the way. Not just for Marcus, not just for the church, but for anyone who wants faith to mean more than politics ever could.

The next chapter—the only one that matters—gets written by those who are bold enough to choose honestly and love recklessly, no matter the cost.

Stay brave. Stay true—to yourself, your values, and our shared future.

COMING SPRING 2026

BOOK II: "STRANGER IN A FORMERLY FAMILIAR LAND"

Ever come home and realize you don't belong there anymore? That's what happened when I moved back to my hometown, and not because I changed my faith, but because I wasn't willing to convert to a ubiquitous, born-again conservative Christianity that had taken over my town. Suddenly, friends and family looked at me differently, and some treated me like I'd caught something dangerous. The disconnect between what we say and how we live Jesus's teachings became painfully obvious.

ROOTS OF THE JESUS PRINCIPLE

That's when the Jesus Principle took root. It's a compass for surviving when the church resists the very questions Jesus would have welcomed.

Book II is that story: Navigating family dinners with silent stares, finding hope when faith communities close ranks, and learning that real Christianity costs you comfort but leads to something better. This isn't just theology—it's survival.

In honest detail, I show how the Jesus Principle pulled me through, guiding me to costly but authentic faith. It's the account of how four simple questions became my compass through the pain of watching people I love choose tribe over truth, politics over compassion, and fear over the radical love Jesus taught.

WHAT'S NEXT

This upcoming volume won't dodge controversy. I'll be tackling hot-button topics like biblical inerrancy, human sexuality, and why so many believers discount science in favor of tribal stories.

The Jesus Principle cuts through assumptions and easy answers, inviting readers into the messy work of faith, belonging, and truth, without sacrificing intellectual honesty or compassion.

COMING SUMMER 2026

BOOK III: "DECONSTRUCTING TOXIC FAITH & RESTORING THE WAY OF JESUS"

The final book in the Jesus Principle Trilogy takes on the biggest challenge yet: tearing down toxic theology and rebuilding faith from the ground up, centered not on culture war slogans, but on the true hope and justice of Jesus.

This isn't soft reform. It's a call to reject beliefs that harm and exclude, and to build a church that actually looks like Christ in Matthew 25: a faith that unites, heals, and risks real change. The world doesn't need more talk about love. It needs more people who practice it, especially when it costs.

THE STAKES KEEP GETTING HIGHER

Meanwhile, the urgency just builds. Trump's rollback of environmental protections, travel bans, the absence of climate action, civil liberties under threat, economic insecurity, and gun deaths—especially for children—are all driven by policies cheered on by conservative Christians.

Social cuts keep hammering the most vulnerable. The central question is brutal: Do these choices reflect the heart of Jesus—or betray it? If faith can't face up to the harm done in its name, it's just noise.

No easy answers here, just honest questions and a path to deeper courage, for those willing to confront both the cost and necessity of change.

YOUR JOURNEY CONTINUES

Marcus chose in that parking lot. I've faced my own crossroads in hard family talks and strained friendships. The Jesus Principle became the lens, painful, but clarifying.

Now it's your turn. Join the ongoing conversation at TheJesusPrinciple.com and on TheJesusPrinciple.substack.com.

The questions haven't gone away. Neither has the choice. A future built on comfort is already dying; a future built on risk and truth is waiting for those willing to step up and face it.

Thank you for reading *The Jesus Principle!*

If this book spoke to you, please take a moment to share your thoughts with others. Even a few words help more readers find it.

THEJESUSPRINCIPLE.COM/LEAVE-A-REVIEW

Your voice matters—and your support makes a real difference.

www.ingramcontent.com/pod-product-compliance
Lightning Source LLC
Chambersburg PA
CBHW070143080526
44586CB00015B/1812